LULU

A sex tragedy

Adapted by
Peter Barnes

from Frank Wedekind's
EARTH SPIRIT and PANDORA'S BOX

Translation by
Charlotte Beck

with an Introduction by
Martin Esslin

 Heinemann London

Heinemann Educational Books Ltd
LONDON EDINBURGH MELBOURNE
SINGAPORE JOHANNESBURG
IBADAN HONG KONG NEW DELHI
TORONTO AUCKLAND
NAIROBI

ISBN 0 435 23059 x (cased)
0 435 23060 3 (paperback)

**All rights whatsoever in this play are strictly
reserved and applications for permission to
perform the play must be made, before rehearsals
commence, to Margaret Ramsay Ltd, 14a Goodwin's
Court, London W.C.2. No performance may be given
unless a licence has been obtained.**

H.17 JAN 1974

Published by
Heinemann Educational Books Ltd
48 Charles Street, London W1X 8AH
Printed in Great Britain by
Morrison & Gibb Ltd, London and Edinburgh

Introduction

Of the creators of modern drama – Ibsen, Strindberg, Haupt-
mann, Wedekind, Chekhov, Pirandello, Shaw and Brecht –
Frank Wedekind is the one who is least known in the English-
speaking world. Yet this neglect is quite undeserved: Wedekind
was decades ahead of his time and his work has dated much less
than much of that of his contemporaries; his grotesque sense of
humour, his love of situations from the world of the police
gazette, the circus or artistic Bohemia (which makes him a
predecessor of pop art) link him directly to present-day trends;
and as a moralist he is right up to date – if Ibsen's Nora is a
suffragette of the nineties, Wedekind's Lulu is a champion of
the nineteen-seventy brand of Women's Liberation.

Wedekind's life (1864–1918) resembles one of his own
grotesquely extravagant plots. His father was a German doctor
who had been physician to the Sultan of Turkey, had then taken
an active part in the Revolution of 1848 and fled to the United
States when it collapsed. In San Francisco he had married a
Hungarian singer at the local German Opera House; their son
narrowly missed being born in America and as a tribute to the
place of his conception his parents gave him an Anglo-Saxon
name – Frank.

Young Frank was as adventurous as his father. He started life
as a journalist, was for a time chief of publicity for a firm of
producers of meat cubes in Switzerland (the brand, *Maggi*, still
exists), then became secretary to a circus with which he travelled
through Europe. He spent some time in London in 1894.
Shortly afterwards, in Paris, he became secretary to the Danish
painter Willi Grétor, one of the greatest art-forgers of history.
More and more drawn to the theatre, he gave recitations of

Ibsen's plays under the pseudonym, Cornelius Minehaha. In 1896, in Munich, he met Frieda Strindberg, who was in the course of divorce proceedings against her husband August Strindberg and bore Wedekind a son – one of the strangest links between great dramatists!

In Munich Wedekind became one of the leaders of the circle round the satirical magazine, *Simplizissimus*, the focal point of a radical, revolutionary intellectual *avant-garde* that poured scorn on the stuffiness of Imperial Germany. And, having already written a number of plays, he also gravitated towards the theatre: as a literary manager, director and actor. In the famous Munich cabaret, *Elf Scharfrichter* (The Eleven Hangmen), he sang his own ballads to the guitar.

The play here published under the title *Lulu* was written between 1892 and 1894. Wedekind himself called it *Pandora's Box*. But his publisher would not take the risk of publishing the last two acts – the gaming scene and Lulu's life in the London attic. So Wedekind divided the immensely long play into two parts and published part one under the title *Der Erdgeist* (The Earth Spirit). This comprised the action up to the murder of Dr Schön. The final two acts, expanded by a third which preceded them, appeared seven years later under the original title *Pandora's Box*.

Thus the division of the play into two – which has militated against its success on the stage—was the result of difficulties with censorship. The first part, *Erdgeist*, could be performed and received its *première* at Leipzig in February 1898. When it became clear that no actor wanted to play the part of Dr Schön Wedekind had decided to try his hand at professional acting and so made his début in it. The play achieved immediate success, while the second part could not be publicly performed at all and had to be relegated to occasional private performances. The first of these was at Nuremberg in 1904; yet the second private performance of *Pandora's Box* on 29 May 1905 in Vienna was the most memorable: Tilly Newes (whom Wedekind married in 1906 and who survived him by more than half a century; she died in 1969) played Lulu, the great Austrian satirist Karl Kraus appeared as the Crown Prince of Uahabee, and Wedekind himself as Jack the Ripper.

It was only after the First World War and Wedekind's death that *Pandora's Box* could be publicly performed. Wedekind himself had tried to make an adaptation of the two plays for one evening in 1913, which left the last scene out; but not even this version could be performed in his lifetime.

This long and tormented history fully justifies Peter Barnes' attempt to produce an actable version for one evening which preserves the main line of the action without suppressing the crucial final scene which Wedekind himself had to omit in his condensed adaptation.

Indeed, there is evidence to show that Wedekind's whole conception stemmed from the character of Jack the Ripper. From the murderer his imagination was drawn to the victim; here lies the origin of the character of Lulu.

What is the subject matter of *Lulu*?

In this and in all his other works Wedekind was one of the pioneers of the struggle against the Victorian conception of sex as something filthy and unclean. He battled against the hypocrisy of the Victorian era which made the intelligent and free discussion of sexual problems impossible. In *Spring's Awakening* he showed how children who have been denied even the most elementary knowledge of the fact of life are driven to furtive sexual acts and to disaster and tragedy through sheer ignorance and frustration.

And as far as *Lulu* is concerned, Wedekind himself has said that he might have given the play the title *Realpsychologie* (real psychology) in 'the same sense in which we speak of *Realpolitik* (realistic politics). In writing the play I was concerned to eliminate all concepts which are logically untenable, concepts such as Love, Faithfulness, Gratitude. The two main characters [of Part One] Schön and Lulu have nothing to do with these concepts even subjectively: she, because she has had no education; he because he has transcended his education.'

In other words: Wedekind wanted to show the sexual impulse as it really is, beyond the value judgements of conventional morals. Admittedly, Lulu who embodies the sexual impulse, leads all who come in touch with her to disaster and ends in disaster herself. But only – and here lies the real message of the play – because society, and its conventional codes and concepts, does not allow the sexual impulse – a woman's sexual impulse – to develop freely and untrammelled. Society's double standard allows the men in Lulu's life to indulge in the wildest promiscuity. But the only man whom Lulu really loves, Dr Schön, refuses to marry her because he feels he needs a 'respectable' wife; and when in the end he realizes that he cannot live without Lulu and *does* marry her after all, his inability to apply his own standards to a woman drives him to his death.

Lulu thus is anything but a *femme fatale*, or the eternal prostitute: she is the most *innocent* character in the play, a human being who simply acts with total sincerity in following her own nature. Her naturalness and innocence expose the distortions of bourgeois morality.

Peter Barnes' adaptation has, I believe, succeeded in fully preserving Wedekind's original intention, while compressing the action into the span of a single evening's performance. In this form *Lulu* should now be able to attain the position in the modern repertoire which the play deserves as a masterpiece of theatrical craftsmanship and a moving statement of an eternal human problem.

MARTIN ESSLIN

Lulu was first presented at Nottingham Playhouse on 7 October 1970 with the following cast:

RINGMASTER	*John Manford*
LULU	*Julia Foster*
SCHÖN	*Jack Allen*
SCHWARZ	*Michael Byrne*
DR GOLL	*Francis Thomas*
ALWA	*Trevor T. Smith*
SCHIGOLCH	*Frederick Bennett*
ESCHERICH	*Geoffrey Bateman*
PRINCE ESCERNY	*Ian White*
HENRIETTE	*Marilyn Fridjon*
COUNTESS GESCHWITZ	*Sheila Ballantine*
HUGENBURG	*Joe Blatchley*
RODRIGO QUAST	*John Turner*
FERDINAND	*John Manford*
BIANETTA	*Marilyn Fridjon*
LUDMILLA	*Susan Brett*
CASTI-PIANI	*Tenniel Evans*
MAGELONE	*Lois Baxter*
KADIDJA	*Jo Garrity*
HEILMAN	*Francis Thomas*
PUNTSCHU	*Ian White*
BOB	*Geoffrey Lightfoot*
POLICEMAN	*Joe Blatchley*
HUNIDEI	*Geoffrey Bateman*
KUNGU-POTI	*John Manford*
DR HILTI	*Francis Thomas*
JACK	*Alec Heggie*

Lulu was subsequently transferred to The Royal Court Theatre, London, on 8 December 1970 with the following cast:

RINGMASTER	*Chris Malcolm*
LULU	*Julia Foster*
SCHÖN	*John Phillips*
SCHWARZ	*Michael Byrne*
DR GOLL	*Francis Thomas*
ALWA	*Edward Petherbridge*
SCHIGOLCH	*Gordon Whiting*
ESCHERICH	*John Grillo*
PRINCE ESCERNY	*John Justin*
HENRIETTE	*Maryilyn Fridjon*
COUNTESS GESCHWITZ	*Sheila Ballantine*
HUGENBURG	*Tom Owen*
RODRIGO QUAST	*John Turner*
FERDINAND	*Chris Malcolm*
BIANETTA	*Marilyn Fridjon*
LUDMILLA	*Susan Brett*
CASTI-PIANI	*Leonard Kavanagh*
MAGELONE	*Maggy Maxwell*
KADIDJA	*Jo Garrity*
HEILMAN	*Francis Thomas*
PUNTSCHU	*John Justin*
BOB	*Paul Hennen*
POLICEMAN	*Chris Malcolm*
HUNIDEI	*John Grillo*
KUNGU-POTI	*Chris Malcolm*
DR HILTI	*Francis Thomas*
JACK	*Michael Byrne*

The Production both at Nottingham
and in London was
Directed by PETER BARNES and STUART BURGE
Designed by Patrick Robertson
Costumes by Rosemary Vercoe
Choreography by Eleanor Fazan
Lighting by Rory Dempster

To Stuart

CHARACTERS

in order of appearance

RINGMASTER
LULU
SCHÖN
SCHWARZ
DR GOLL
ALWA
SCHIGOLCH
ESCHERICH *a reporter*
PRINCE ESCERNY
HENRIETTE *a maid*
COUNTESS GESCHWITZ
HUGENBURG *a schoolboy*
RODRIGO QUAST *an acrobat*
FERDINAND *a gamekeeper*
BIANETTA *a courtesan*
LUDMILLA *a courtesan*
CASTI-PIANI
MAGELONE *a music hall artist*
KADIDJA *her daughter*
HEILMAN *a newspaperman*
PUNTSCHU *a financier*
BOB *a pageboy*
POLICEMAN
HUNIDEI
KUNGU-POTI
DR HILTI
JACK

ACT ONE   BERLIN
ACT TWO   Scene 1 BERLIN
          Scene 2 PARIS
          Scene 3 LONDON

PROLOGUE

Coloured lights, loud circus fanfare and music and the RINGMASTER *with a whip and firing a gun, strides down the centre gangway shouting through a megaphone.*

RINGMASTER: Roll up! Roll up! Ladies and Gentlemen, and see the wild animals! Excitement! Thrills! Danger! The greatest show on Earth! Roll up! Roll up! Roll up!

He leaps on to the stage and cracks his whip.

Step inside, we have tigers, monkeys, bears, and just behind the curtains there's a camel. Reptiles too: chameleons, salamanders, snakes, you don't believe me? – wait.

He cracks his whip; the curtain parts slightly to show a burly ASSISTANT *standing beside a cage. Inside the cage is the actress playing* LULU *dressed in a glittering, skin-tight, one-piece suit.*

The RINGMASTER *cracks his whip again; the* ASSISTANT *opens the cage and takes* LULU *out: she coils herself sinuously around his body.*

> She's made to dazzle and delight
> Out here she's harmless but step inside
> And see her fight a tiger.
> She'll coil herself around him,
> He'll roar – who'll win?
> Step inside and see the wild animals.

Another crack of the whip and the ASSISTANT *puts* LULU *back into the cage. The* RINGMASTER *strokes her legs as she passes, cooing gently to her. The curtain closes. The* RINGMASTER *faces the audience.*

> And that's not all.
> See me place my head into the beast's stinking jaw.
> I'm not afraid it holds my head in awe,
> Until I crack a joke, then it bites.

But I will set a joke against my life.
Step inside and see the wild animals!

He gestures. Curtain up. Music held for a moment, then fades down. The RINGMASTER *exits Wings Right.*

ACT ONE

SCENE ONE

A large studio with entrance door Up Stage Centre. Stage Right door to the bedroom. Centre Stage a platform for the model. Down Stage Left, two easels. On the far one a head and shoulder portrait of a young girl. Another canvas rests against the front easel, its reverse side facing the audience. Down Stage off Centre an ottoman with a tiger skin over it.

SCHÖN *sits stiffly on the edge of the ottoman inspecting the portrait of the girl on the far easel. Brush and palette in hand* SCHWARZ *stands beside it.*

SCHÖN: Is that really how you see her?

SCHWARZ: The secret is to create a peaceful atmosphere during the sitting. I make her relax.

SCHÖN: Ah, now I understand why she looks different.

SCHWARZ: Step over there, you'll get a better view.

SCHÖN (*in crossing, knocks over the other easel*): I'm sorry. . . .

SCHWARZ (*picking it up*): That's all right.

SCHÖN (*disturbed*): What's this . . .?

    SCHWARZ *stands the painting on the easel. It is of a woman dressed as Pierrot with a long shepherd's staff in her hands.*

SCHWARZ: A costume piece.

SCHON: You've certainly made a success of *her.*

SCHWARZ: Do you know her then?

SCHÖN: No. And even if I did how could I recognize her in that costume?

SCHWARZ: It's not finished yet. What can you expect. While she's posing I have to keep her husband entertained as well.

SCHÖN: How do you do that?

SCHWARZ (*grimacing*): By talking about ART . . . she seems to melt into that ridiculous costume – the way she has of burying her arms in her pockets.

3

SCHÖN: It's all in the painting.

SCHWARZ: Would you like to meet her?

SCHÖN: No.

SCHWARZ: She should be here any minute.

    SCHÖN *hurriedly picks up his gloves and silver-topped cane.*

SCHÖN: How many more sittings will there be?

SCHWARZ: I'll probably have to suffer the torments of Tantalus for another three months.

SCHÖN (*gesturing to the other portrait*): No I mean that one.

SCHWARZ: Oh, sorry. Three more at most (*accompanying him to the door*). If the lady could leave her blouse, I'd be able to finish it much quicker.

SCHÖN (*nodding*): Of course. . . .

    SCHWARZ *opens the door and they collide with* LULU *and* DR GOLL, *a fat man with a tight collar, shiny black hair and short of breath.*

    Good God . . .

SCHWARZ: May I introduce . . .

SCHÖN (*kissing* LULU'S *hand*): Madame Goll.

    SCHWARZ *looks surprised.*

GOLL: What are you doing here?

SCHÖN: Looking at a painting of my fiancée.

LULU (*coming Down Stage*): Is she here?

SCHÖN: No (*gesturing*). That's her portrait.

LULU: She's lovely.

SCHÖN: She usually has her sittings in the afternoon.

GOLL: Why are you keeping it a secret?

LULU (*pulling a face*): Is she always so serious?

SCHÖN: The after-effect of finishing school.

GOLL (*in front of the portrait*): Yes anyone can see she's been through a lot.

SCHÖN: I'm going to announce our engagement in a fortnight. She's going to make a new man of me.

GOLL (*to* LULU): We're wasting time! Come on . . .! (SCHÖN *prepares to leave.*) No wait. We must talk. Get a move on Nellie. Rembrandt here's licking his brushes.

LULU (*petulantly*): I thought this was going to be fun.

SCHÖN: You'd give us all a great deal of pleasure.

LULU (*eagerly*): Just you wait.

> LULU *goes into the bedroom Right and* SCHWARZ *stands guard in front of the door.*

GOLL: I called her Nellie on our marriage licence.

SCHÖN: Why don't you call her Mignon?

GOLL: I never thought of it.

SCHÖN: You think a name's important?

GOLL: I haven't any children.

SCHÖN: You've only been married a few months.

GOLL: I don't want any!

SCHÖN: Madame Goll seems to be taking her time.

GOLL: No, she's as quick as lightning. Dressing and undressing – women have to be virtuosos the same as we all have to be in our different ways if we want to earn a living. *Nellie!* . . .

SCHWARZ (*knocking on the door*): Madame Goll.

LULU (*from inside*): Coming. Coming.

GOLL (*to* SCHÖN, *gesturing discreetly to* SCHWARZ): They're cold fishes.

SCHÖN: I envy them. They believe there's something holy in starving. (*Smiles thinly.*) Anyway one shouldn't pass an opinion on a man who's lived from hand to palette since childhood. Why don't you finance him, Goll? It'd just be a minor problem in accountancy for you.

> LULU *enters in the Pierrot costume.*

LULU: Here I am.

SCHÖN (*turning: a pause*): Superb.

LULU (*curtsying*): Well?

SCHÖN: Art must despair before you.

GOLL: You thinks so too. I've never seen a skin as white as hers. But I've told Raphael here to spare the flesh tones. I don't admire these modern daubs.

SCHWARZ: Thanks to the Impressionists Modern Art can stand comparison with the Old Masters.

GOLL: To decorate slaughterhouse walls! For *cattle*!

SCHÖN: Don't excite yourself.

> LULU *throws her arms round* GOLL'S *neck and kisses him.*

5

GOLL: Your slip's showing!

LULU: I wanted to leave it off, Buzzi.

She picks up a shepherd's staff on the platform.

GOLL (*sitting down, Stage Right*): Come over here. This is my observation post.

SCHWARZ: The light's good today.

GOLL: Come on now. Get her down on canvas. Bold strokes!

SCHWARZ: Certainly, Dr Goll.

GOLL: Be perfectly natural, Nellie. . . . Act as if Velasquez here didn't exist.

LULU: Painters aren't really men anyhow.

SCHÖN: Don't judge the whole tribe by one illustrious exception.

A knock. SCHWARZ *crosses to open the door.*

GOLL (*to* LULU: *gesturing to* SCHWARZ): You can smile at him if you want to. It's quite safe.

SCHÖN: It makes no difference to him if she smiles or not.

GOLL: And what if it did? That's why I'm sitting here. To make sure it doesn't make any difference.

SCHWARZ *opens the door;* ALWA *enters.*

ALWA: Father are you ready? (*Sees* LULU.) *You?* You look wonderful.

SCHÖN: Alwa. Dr Goll, you know my son.

ALWA *crosses and shakes hands with* GOLL.

ALWA: Dr Goll. . . . (*to* LULU) If only I could get you as my leading lady.

LULU: I don't think I dance well enough for your ballet.

SCHÖN: What brings you here?

ALWA: I want to take you to my dress rehearsal.

SCHÖN *nods and gets up.*

GOLL: What's the title of this ballet of yours?

ALWA: 'The Dalai Lama.'

GOLL: Dalai Lama, isn't he in a lunatic asylum?

SCHÖN: You're thinking of Nietsche.

GOLL: Oh yes Nietsche. Of course it's Nietsche who's in an asylum.

ALWA: My ballet will put Buddhism back on its feet. Please join us, Doctor.

6

GOLL: No. It's impossible.

ALWA: You'll like the Third Act . . . The Dalai Lama surrounded by her young monks. You'll see our monkeys, our Brahmins and our little girls.

GOLL: *Little girls* . . . no don't tempt me . . . how can I go? By the time I get back Bruegel here'll have made a mess of the whole picture.

ALWA: Gentlemen, the young Brahmins wait impatiently and the daughters of Nirvana stand shivering in their tights.

GOLL: *Tights!?* . . . (*quickly up*) I'll be back in five minutes.

He crosses and compares the portrait with LULU.

ALWA (*bowing to* LULU): I'm sorry.

GOLL (*to* SCHWARZ): It needs more modelling here. The hair's bad. You're not paying enough attention. Concentrate . . .! (*He follows the others to the door.*) Concentrate . . .! Concentrate . . .!

They exit.

SCHWARZ (*spitting after them*): Scum . . .! A man must eat but he has to be broken first. (*He studies* LULU.) Please raise your right hand a little, Madame.

LULU (*lifts her crook as high as she can*): Who'd have thought he'd have left me alone . . .

SCHWARZ: I suppose you think I'm ridiculous?

LULU (*anxiously*): He's coming right back.

SCHWARZ: Can you really dance? (LULU *nods*.) Who teaches you?

LULU: He does. He plays the violin.

SCHWARZ: One learns something new every day . . . Don't you feel cold?

LULU: No why? Are you cold?

SCHWARZ: Not today.

LULU *breathes deeply.*

Stop it!

LULU: I didn't mean to hurt your feelings before.

SCHWARZ: If you would . . . the left leg . . . a little higher . . . (*Crosses to dais.*) If you'll let me . . . You're nervous . . .

He tries to touch her; she throws the shepherd's crook in his face.

LULU: Leave me alone!

7

SCHWARZ: It was only a joke.

LULU: *A joke!* Just leave me alone!

She darts behind the ottoman, he edges around after her.

SCHWARZ: After I've punished you.

LULU: You'll have to catch me first!

SCHWARZ (*diving over the ottoman*): Got you!

LULU (*throwing the tiger skin over his head*): Sweet dreams!

She rushes to the easel as he disentangles himself.

SCHWARZ: All right let's make up.

He makes a sudden lunge for her as she smashes the portrait of SCHÖN's *fiancée over his head.*

SCHWARZ (*horrified*): *Arrrrrrrrhhhh!*

LULU: It's your fault.

SCHWARZ: I'm ruined! Ten weeks work. My exhibition . . . (*savagely*) Right. Now I've nothing more to lose!

He rushes after her and trips over the easel as she stamps savagely on the portrait.

LULU: So she's made a new man of him!

SCHWARZ (*staggering up*): No quarter!

LULU: I'm dizzy . . .

She falls seductively on to the floor. SCHWARZ *hesitates, then bolts the door, lies down beside her and kisses her.*

SCHWARZ: I love you.

LULU: I loved a student once.

SCHWARZ: Nellie . . .

LULU: He had twenty-four duelling scars.

SCHWARZ: I love you, Nellie.

LULU: My name isn't Nellie. (*He kisses her.*) It's Lulu.

SCHWARZ: I'll call you Eve.

LULU *lifts his head and kisses him.*

LULU: You stink of tobacco.

SCHWARZ (*jumping up distraught*): God Almighty, what am I doing . . .

LULU (*up*): Don't kill me . . .!

SCHWARZ: You've never been in love.

LULU: You're the one who's never been in love.

A loud banging on the entrance door.

GOLL (*off*): Open the door!

LULU: Hide me!

   SCHWARZ *wants to go to the door but* LULU *holds him back amid the loud battering.*

He'll beat me to death!

GOLL: Open the door! Open the door!

LULU: He'll kill me! He'll kill me!

   The whole door suddenly falls in with a crash, amid a cloud of dust. GOLL *stands momentarily in the doorway, neck muscles bulging. He rushes in with bull-like roars, flaying the air with his walking stick.*

GOLL (*yelling*): Pigs . . .! Filth . . .! You . . .!

   He suddenly gasps loudly. His head jerks back convulsively, his wig falls off; clutching his chest he collapses.

   LULU *has run to the door.* SCHWARZ *tentatively approaches the prostrate* GOLL.

SCHWARZ: Dr Goll . . .

LULU: You'd better tidy up the studio. It's a mess.

SCHWARZ: Help me get him on to the ottoman.

LULU: We couldn't lift him.

SCHWARZ: I'll get a doctor. (*He crosses, pauses in the doorway and looks round.*) You're right, the place is in a mess. Try and clear it up before I come back with somebody.

   He exits. LULU *approaches* GOLL'S *body fearfully.*

LULU: Buzzi . . . Sweet . . . his eyes are following me . . . he's looking at my legs. . . . (*She touches him with her toe.*) Buzzi it's serious . . . no more dancing . . . he's walked out on me . . . now what am I going to do. (*kneeling looking into his face*) I don't recognize you no more, Buzzi . . .

   SCHWARZ *comes back.*

SCHWARZ: The doctor'll be here any minute.

LULU: What am I going to do? What about *me*?

SCHWARZ (*kneeling down beside* GOLL): Dr Goll . . .

LULU: He's snuffed it.

SCHWARZ: Don't be so vulgar.

LULU: He wouldn't have spoken to me like that. (*kneeling on the opposite side of* GOLL) Please close his eyes.

9

SCHWARZ: Don't you feel anything?

LULU: One day it'll be my turn.

SCHWARZ: I'm not listening.

LULU: And one day it'll be your turn. Close his eyes. He's staring at me.

SCHWARZ: He's staring at me too.

LULU: Close his eyes you coward!

Trembling, he closes GOLL'S *eyes.*

SCHWARZ: It's the first time in my life I've ever had to do that.

LULU: Didn't you do it for your mother?

SCHWARZ: No. . . .

LULU: You were scared?

SCHWARZ: NO!

LULU: I didn't mean anything.

SCHWARZ: It so happens she's still alive.

LULU (*brightly*): Oh then you've got somebody who cares for you.

SCHWARZ: No. She's as poor as a beggar.

LULU: I know what that's like. . . . Now I'll be rich.

SCHWARZ *takes her hand, raises her up and steers her to the ottoman.*

SCHWARZ: Look into my eyes. What do you see?

LULU (*looking*): Me, dressed as Pierrot.

SCHWARZ: I'm going to ask one question. Can you answer truthfully . . .?

LULU: I don't know.

SCHWARZ: Is there anything you can swear by?

LULU: I don't know.

SCHWARZ: Do you believe in God?

LULU: I don't know.

SCHWARZ: What do you believe in?

LULU: I don't know.

SCHWARZ: *Have you ever been in love?*

LULU: I don't know.

SCHWARZ (*looking at* GOLL): He knows.

LULU (*rising*): But I don't know. What do you want?

SCHWARZ: Go and get dressed!

Shrugging, LULU *goes into the bedroom.* SCHWARZ *picks up*

10

GOLL'S *wig and kneels beside the corpse. Lights down to a Spot on him Down Stage Centre.*

SCHWARZ: I'll change places with you. I've no courage left. I've had to wait too long. I'm not used to being happy. Wake up. I haven't touched her. . . . (*Tenderly puts* GOLL'S *wig back over his face.*) God, let me be happy. Give me the strength to be happy for her sake.

Spot up on bedroom door, as LULU *comes out in a white silk negligee.*

LULU: Will somebody button me up? My hands are trembling.

SCHWARZ'S *Spot immediately out. Circus music comes up loudly.*

SCENE TWO

A set of large mirrors are lowered on a diagonal Stage Right to form a curving wall. LULU *walks slowly Down Stage in front of them, never taking her eyes off her reflection. She stops at the end mirror Down Stage Right. She regards herself critically, then satisfied turns away. Music starts fading out, mirrors taken up as she moves off.*

Lights up on an elegant drawing room. Door Up Stage Centre. Up Stage Right the fireplace, and above it a portrait of Lulu. Stage Left and Right doorways with a couple of steps leading up to them. Chairs and a table Stage Centre with a small box, decanter and mail on a tray.

LULU *lies full length on the chaise-longue, yawning.* SCHWARZ *enters Right.*

SCHWARZ: Eve. . . .

LULU (*smiling*): At your service.

SCHWARZ: You look beautiful.

LULU: It depends on what you expect.

SCHWARZ (*kissing her*): I've a lot of work to do today.

LULU: You just think you have.

SCHWARZ *crosses and picks up some letters on the table.*

SCHWARZ: Every morning I wake up frightened our world'll collapse. (*Returns, reading a letter.*) My painting of the Sama-

queca dancer went for 50,000 marks. That's the third picture
I've sold since we were married.

LULU: And there's more to come.

SCHWARZ: Look . . . (*hands* LULU *an invitation*).

LULU (*reads*): 'Heinrich Ritter von Zarnikov has the honour to
announce the engagement of his daughter Charlotte Marie
Adelaide to Ludwig Schön.'

SCHWARZ: So he's finally announced the engagement. I've
never understood the delay. There couldn't have been any
obstacles for a man with his influence. (*Moving away.*) And now
to work. . . . (*Turns back.*) Eve . . .

LULU (*smiling*): At your service.

SCHWARZ (*coming back sitting beside her*): Every day it's as if I see
you for the first time.

LULU (*stroking his hair*): You're wasting me.

SCHWARZ: Well, you're mine, aren't you?

   They kiss. A doorbell rings off.

SCHWARZ: Damn!

LULU (*yelling*): Nobody home!

SCHWARZ: Perhaps it's an art dealer.

LULU: Or the Emperor of China.

SCHWARZ: Where's Henriette?

LULU: She's out.

SCHWARZ: Just a minute.

   He exits Up Stage.

LULU (*lays back as if seeing a vision*): Is it him?

   SCHWARZ *returns.*

SCHWARZ: It's only a tramp. I haven't any change. Would you
deal with him? It's time I started work.

   As he exits Stage Right, the seedy figure of SCHIGOLCH *peers
round the doorpost and shuffles in scratching himself.* LULU *does not
turn round.*

SCHIGOLCH: I thought he'd be more of a gent.

LULU: How *could* you ask him for money?

SCHIGOLCH: It's what I dragged my bones here for. You said
he spent the morning painting.

LULU: He overslept. How much?

SCHIGOLCH: Two hundred if you got that much handy. Three hundred'd be even better.

LULU goes to the table, unlocks the small box and takes out some money. SCHIGOLCH *looks round.*

I wanted to see what you're new home looked like . . . It's wonderful. Just like the place I had fifty years ago. You've come a long way! (*feeling the sofa*). Real silk, eh? . . . Lovely.

LULU (*giving him the money*): I love feeling it against my skin.

SCHIGOLCH (*gazing at* LULU'S *portrait*): Is that you?

LULU pours two drinks.

LULU: Good isn't it?

SCHIGOLCH (*shrugging*): It makes you happy . . . (*Sees* LULU *pouring drinks.*) Ahh . . . Does he drink much?

LULU: Not yet. Drink affects everyone differently. It just makes him go to sleep. (*They cross to the ottoman and sit.*) What's been happening?

SCHIGOLCH: Nothing 'cept the streets get longer and my legs get shorter.

LULU: I was beginning to think you were dead.

SCHIGOLCH: I thought so too. (*coughing*) Winter'll do the trick. (*Strokes* LULU'S *thighs.*) And what about my little Lulu?

LULU: It's funny you calling me Lulu. Lulu sounds out of date. My name's Eve now.

SCHIGOLCH (*licking his glass*): Lulu . . . Eve . . . what's the difference? All this luxury fit for a queen.

LULU (*shuddering*): When I look back . . . !

SCHIGOLCH (*stroking her knee*): What do you do all day? Are you still learning French?

LULU: I lie around and sleep.

SCHIGOLCH: That shows you've got class. What else?

LULU (*stretching sinuously*): I stretch till my bones crack.

SCHIGOLCH: L – o – v – e – l – y bones . . . and after . . .

LULU: Why should you care?

SCHIGOLCH: Why should I care? I can't think of my Lulu alone and penniless. I've always had faith in you, Eve, even when you was tiny. Now see what you've become.

LULU (*getting up*): An animal.

SCHIGOLCH: But what an animal. Now I can die in peace. I'll even forgive the undertakers who'll wash me when I'm laid out.

LULU (*sniffing*): There's no need to be afraid of anybody wanting to wash you before you're dead.

SCHIGOLCH: I don't worry about washing.

LULU *has picked up a scent spray from the desk and sprays him with it.*

LULU: A good wash'll bring you back to life.

SCHIGOLCH: We're all filth.

LULU: Not me! I use cream and powder every day.

SCHIGOLCH: In your case it's probably worth it.

LULU (*feeling her arms*): It makes my skin soft as satin.

SCHIGOLCH: We're still filth.

LULU: Speak for yourself. I want to be good enough to eat.

SCHIGOLCH (*rising*): Just you wait, my girl, your admirers won't always think you're such a tasty dish. Whilst there's a bit of go in you it's fine. (*He comes behind her and pulls her hair.*) But afterwards they'll serve up your carcass for dogmeat.

The front doorbell rings off. SCHIGOLCH *shuffles away.*

SCHIGOLCH: I'll find my own way out.

LULU: You've got enough money?

SCHIGOLCH: Enough to buy myself a wreath.

He exits Up Stage Centre at a fast wheezing shuffle. Angry mumbles off. SCHÖN *enters a few second later by the same entrance.*

SCHÖN: Mignon. What's your father doing here? If I were your husband he wouldn't be allowed through the door.

LULU: You can call me Lulu if you want. Walter isn't here.

SCHÖN: Thank you for the honour, madame.

LULU: I don't understand you.

SCHÖN: I know. (*indicating chair*) That's what I want to talk to you about.

LULU (*sitting uncertainly*): Why didn't you tell me when I was with you yesterday?

SCHÖN: I told you two years ago.

LULU: Oh that . . .

SCHÖN: You must stop seeing me. Do you understand? (LULU *shakes her head.*) Either you behave yourself or I'll ask your

14

husband to keep a watch on you. (LULU *gets up and shouts off Right*.)

LULU: Walter!

SCHÖN: No!

LULU (*turns triumphant*): Ahhh . . .

SCHÖN: I'm getting you accepted in society. Your name means something. You can be prouder of that than your relationship with me.

LULU *rushes over and puts her arms round* SCHÖN'S *neck*.

LULU: What are you afraid of? You've got what you want.

SCHÖN (*pushing her away*): All I want is to bring my bride back to a respectable home.

LULU: We'll meet when you think best.

SCHÖN: We'll only meet if you're with your husband.

LULU: You don't believe that.

SCHÖN: Your husband's become my friend, thanks to his marriage to you . . . and what I've done for him.

LULU: He's my friend too.

SCHÖN (*sitting on chaise-longue*): Your husband's a child or he'd have seen through your affairs long ago.

LULU: I wish he would. He feels safe because he has a marriage licence in his pocket. He's not a child – he's banal. He sees nothing. Not me or himself. He's blind . . .

SCHÖN (*half to himself*): And when his eyes are opened?

LULU (*eagerly*): You do it! Open his eyes. He's ruining me. I'm neglecting myself. *He makes no demands!* Everything suits him because he's never made love to a woman in his life.

SCHÖN: That can't be true. He's been painting young girls since he was fourteen.

LULU: He's afraid of women. He thinks they undermine his health . . . (*wryly*). But he's not afraid of me.

SCHÖN: Good God lots of women would be overjoyed to be in your place.

LULU (*close to him, wheedling*): Lead him astray please. You know how; you're an expert. Get him into bad company. Introduce him to your friends. I'm only a wife to him and I feel such a fool. He'll be prouder of me afterwards. He doesn't know the difference between me and other women. I've been racking my brains to find a way of shaking him up. One night I even danced the can-can in front of him. All he did was yawn and burble some nonsense about indecency.

SCHÖN: Well after all he is an artist.

LULU: He thinks he is.

SCHÖN: That's the main thing.

LULU: When I sit for him I make him feel he's a great artist.

SCHÖN: He is. I've made him one.

LULU: He's suspicious, but at the same time he lets himself be lied to right and left. One loses all respect. . . . You know on our honeymoon I told him I'd never been with another man. . . .

    SCHÖN *in astonishment.*

If I hadn't he'd have thought I was depraved.

SCHÖN: You demand too much from a legitimate relationship like marriage.

LULU: I often dream about Goll.

SCHÖN: You want to be back under the whip?

LULU: I don't dance any more.

SCHÖN: Ninety women out of a hundred train their husbands into their ways.

LULU: He loves me.

SCHÖN: Ah, that makes it difficult, I'll admit.

LULU: He doesn't know me, but he loves me.

    SCHÖN *gets up.*

SCHÖN: I've married you off twice already. You live in luxury. I've built up your husband's reputation. Now leave me alone!

LULU: If I belong to anyone on earth I belong to you. Without you I'd be . . . I don't know where I'd be. Remember when I tried to steal your watch, you took me in. Anyone else would've called the police. You sent me to school. Taught me how to behave. There's nobody else in the world who cares tuppence about me. I was glad to earn my keep as a dancer and a model. But I can't love to order.

SCHÖN (*voice rising*): I've sacrificed enough already because of my affair with you. I thought you'd be satisfied with a nice healthy young man. If you feel you owe me something, then don't throw yourself at me. What good is it if you're married and still seen coming in and out of my home every hour of the day. Why the devil didn't Goll have the decency to stay alive? He would've kept you under lock and key and I could've brought my wife home long ago!

LULU: She'll soon get on your nerves. She's too unspoilt for your tastes ... I don't mind you getting married ... (*angrily*) But don't treat me like dirt!

SCHÖN: Like dirt? The only thing dirty are your affairs!

SCHWARZ enters Stage Right.

SCHWARZ: What's going on?

LULU (*to* SCHÖN): Tell him.

SCHÖN: Be quiet.

LULU: I've had enough of you two!

She exits Stage Left.

SCHÖN (*to himself*): I must be free ...

SCHWARZ: What's the matter?

SCHÖN indicates a chair, SCHWARZ sits down.

SCHÖN (*awkwardly*): You've been happy the last six months haven't you ...? You've a wife everyone envies but she needs a man she can respect.

SCHWARZ: Doesn't she respect me?

SCHÖN: No.

SCHWARZ (*gloomily*): I came from the bottom and she's from the top. All I want to do is to be worthy of her. (*Extends his hand to* SCHÖN.) Thank you for telling me.

SCHÖN (*shaking his hand, embarrassed*): Oh it's nothing . . . nothing . . .

SCHWARZ: Is there anything else you can tell me?

SCHÖN: Keep watch on her a bit more.

SCHWARZ: Why ...?

SCHÖN: We're not children playing games. This is life. She wants to be taken seriously. She's worth that much.

SCHWARZ (*suspiciously*): What's she been doing?

SCHÖN: Remember how much you have to thank her for and...

SCHWARZ: Who with? Who with?

SCHÖN: I haven't come here to start a scandal but to save myself from one.

SCHWARZ (*shaking his head*): You're mistaken . . . something she's said . . .

SCHÖN: I can't see you living blind. The girl deserves to be made a respectable woman. She's changed for the better since I've known her.

SCHWARZ: Since you've known her. How long's that?

SCHÖN: Since she was twelve. She was a flower girl outside the Alhambra Café.

SCHWARZ: She never told me.

SCHÖN: Quite right. I'm telling you so you'll realize there's no question of moral depravity. On the contrary the girl has exceptional gifts.

SCHWARZ: She told me her aunt brought her up.

SCHÖN: That's the woman I got to look after her. She was her best pupil. Mothers used to hold her up as an example to their daughters.

SCHWARZ (*sobbing*): Oh God . . .

SCHÖN: There's no 'Oh Goding' about it. What's past is past. I'm speaking to you as a friend and I'm offering you my help. Don't let me down.

SCHWARZ *goes progressively to pieces, sitting and standing and making zigzag movements across the room.*

SCHWARZ: She told me she'd never been with another man.

SCHÖN (*exasperated*): But she was a *widow*!

SCHWARZ: He made her wear children's clothes. He treated her like a child.

SCHÖN: But he married her. I still don't know how she made him do it.

SCHWARZ: How did Goll get to know her?

SCHÖN: Through me. After my wife died and I was getting to know my fiancée, she started coming between us.

SCHWARZ (*stops pacing: stares*): And when Goll died? What scheme . . . you . . . she . . . (*Moans.*)

SCHÖN: You married a rich woman and now you're a famous artist. You don't get there without money. Don't sit in judgement. You can't apply the standards of the bourgeois society to a woman with Mignon's background.

SCHWARZ (*confused*): What background?

SCHÖN: Her brutal childhood. With the sort of father she had, it's a miracle she's turned out the way she has – with all her faults.

SCHWARZ: He died in a lunatic asylum didn't he?

SCHÖN: He's just been here.

SCHWARZ (*harsh gurgle*): Her father?

SCHÖN: He tried to slip out when I arrived. Look their glasses are still standing there.

SCHWARZ (*despairing*): She said he'd died in an asylum.

SCHÖN: The whip. All she wants is to obey you. She was blissfully happy with Goll.

SCHWARZ: She said she'd never been with another man. She swore on her mother's grave.

SCHÖN: She never knew her mother. Much less her grave.

SCHWARZ (*covering his eyes with his hands*): Pain . . .

SCHÖN: Hang on to her while she's still yours.

SCHWARZ: If only I could cry. If only I could howl.

> SCHÖN *grabs him.* SCHWARZ *looks up apparently calm.*

You're right, yes you're right . . . (*He moves away.*)

SCHÖN: Where are you going?

SCHWARZ: To talk to her.

SCHÖN: Good.

> SCHWARZ *exits Stage Right.* SCHÖN *crosses to the table to pour himself a drink.*

Difficult job . . . (*Pauses suddenly, looks to door Stage Left.*) Didn't she go in there?

> *Suddenly loud groans come from Stage Right.* SCHÖN *hurries over and finds the door locked; rattling it.*

Herr Schwarz . . . Walter . . .

> LULU *enters in a white dress Stage Left as groans and cries continue.*

LULU: What's that?

SCHÖN: Is there an axe in the kitchen? I don't want to kick it in . . .

LULU: He'll open it when he's finished crying.

SCHÖN (*still banging on the door*): Get the axe!

The front doorbell rings in the corridor. LULU *and* SCHÖN *stare at each other.*

I can't be seen here . . .

As he creeps to the Up Stage entrance, the door bursts open and ALWA *enters, excited.*

ALWA: Father, there's been a revolution in Paris!

A great cry is heard off Stage Right. SCHÖN *and* LULU *stare and rush back.*

SCHÖN: Walter! Walter!

LULU: Merciful God!

SCHÖN: Get that axe!

LULU *hurries off Up Stage.* SCHÖN *continues banging at the door.*

ALWA: He's just play acting.

SCHÖN (*suddenly*): Did you say there's been a revolution in Paris?

ALWA: You should see the office. They've gone berserk. Nobody knows what to write. You'd better get down there.

SCHÖN (*kicking the door in rage*): Walter!

ALWA: Shall I break it down?

SCHÖN: She enjoys herself and leaves us to take the consequences. Walter!

LULU *returns with an axe.*

LULU: Henriette's just come back.

SCHÖN: Shut the door behind you then.

As LULU *closes the Up Stage door* ALWA *grabs the axe from her and strikes the door Stage Right.*

SCHÖN: Harder!

ALWA *strikes again, the door flies open.* ALWA *looks inside and staggers back in horror dropping the axe. A pause.* LULU *indicates the open doorway.*

LULU (*to* SCHÖN): After you . . .

SCHÖN *straightens up determinedly and marches in. With her hand on her mouth,* LULU *goes up the steps to the doorway. She looks in and steadies herself against the door-post; then rushes across to* ALWA *slumped in the chaise-longue.*

I can't stay here. (*She pulls him up.*) And I can't be alone.

She exits Left dragging ALWA *with her as* SCHÖN *returns. There is blood on his hands. Acting calmly, he pulls the door shut behind him, goes to the table and quickly writes two short notes as* ALWA *returns.*

SCHÖN: Where is she?

ALWA: In her room changing.

SCHÖN *folds the two notes and rings a tiny handbell. The maid* HENRIETTE *enters.*

SCHÖN (*handing her a note*): Take this note to Dr Bernstein . . . (*handing her a second note*) and this one to the police. Take a cab. Hurry . . .

HENRIETTE *exits.*

ALWA: I'm always paralysed by the sight of blood.

SCHÖN: The *idiot*!

ALWA: I suppose he finally woke up.

SCHÖN: He was too self-centred.

LULU *appears in the doorway Left in black coat and large black hat.*

ALWA: Where are you going?

LULU: Out. I can see blood everywhere. You must write the obituary yourself. Call him another Michaelangelo.

SCHÖN (*savagely*): What's the good of that? My marriage is lying dead and cold in there.

ALWA: It's a kind of poetic justice.

SCHÖN: Why don't you shout it in the streets?

ALWA (*gesturing to* LULU): After mother died, you should have done the right thing by her.

SCHÖN: In an hour's time they'll be selling special editions. 'Leading Newspaper Proprietor and Dead Artist's Wife.' I won't be able to show my face.

LULU: It's not your fault.

SCHÖN: That's exactly why they'll crucify me.

ALWA: Go away then.

SCHÖN: And let the scandal spread?

LULU (*touching the chaise-longue*): Ten minutes ago he was sitting there. (ALWA *jumps up*)

SCHÖN: This is the thanks I get. He's ruined my life in one

irresponsible moment. (*to* LULU) What are you going to tell the police?

LULU: Nothing. He was always getting these suicidal fits.

SCHÖN: He had everything a man could want.

ALWA: He paid a high price for it.

SCHÖN (*flaring up*): I know what your idea is. You want to make sure you're my only heir. Well, that's why I'm going to marry again.

ALWA: You always were a poor judge of character.

LULU (*brightly*): Why don't you bring out your own special edition? 'Artist Friend of Newspaper Proprietor Kills Himself.'

SCHÖN: Him and his damn conscience. (*He has a sudden thought.*) Did you say there's been a revolution in Paris?

ALWA (*nodding*): The editorial staff were taken completely by surprise.

SCHÖN (*thoughtfully*): Good . . . Good . . . a revolution's bigger than a suicide. Artists are killing themselves every day.

The bell rings in the corridor.

ALWA: The police . . .

He exits Up Stage. SCHÖN *is about to follow.* LULU *stops him.*

LULU: There's blood on you.

She sprays her handkerchief with scent and wipes SCHÖN'S *hand.*

LULU: It doesn't leave a stain.

SCHÖN: You monster.

LULU: But you'll marry me in the end.

ALWA *comes in with* ESCHERICH, *a small, confident figure.*

ESCHERICH (*breathless*): Been running . . . all way . . . from police station . . . introduce myself . . . (*Hands* SCHÖN *his card.*)

SCHÖN (*reading card*): Fritz Escherich, reporter.

ESCHERICH: It's a suicide I hear.

ALWA *and* LULU *exit Up Stage as* ESCHERICH *takes out a notebook and pencil and goes round the room making notes.*

ESCHERICH: Door broken . . . kitchen axe . . . (*He bends to pick it up.*)

SCHÖN: I wouldn't touch anything.

ESCHERICH *starts to go into the room Right.* SCHÖN *restrains him.*

SCHÖN: You'd better be prepared.

ESCHERICH (*smugly*): Come, come please open the door.

SCHÖN opens the door. ESCHERICH moves forward. He freezes in the doorway and gives a strangled cry of fright: 'Ahhhhhhhhh.' Dropping his pad, he staggers back clutching his hair.

SCHÖN: Take a good look!

ESCHERICH: C-C-C – Can't . . .

SCHÖN (*pushing him forward contemptuously*): It's what you're paid for!

ESCHERICH (*backing out, feeling his throat*): With a *razor* . . .

Whilst SCHÖN closes the door ESCHERICH staggers to the table to get a drink. SCHÖN picks up his pad and crosses to him.

SCHÖN (*forcing him into a chair*): Sit . . . write . . .

ESCHERICH (*shaking*): C-C-Can't . . .

SCHÖN (*standing behind him*): WRITE . . . (*slowly*) Persecution mania . . .

The lights dim to a Spot on them as ESCHERICH mechanically picks up his pencil.

ESCHERICH (*repeating slowly*): Persecution Mania. (*He starts writing.*) Pers . . . er . . . er . . . pers . . . (*A long pause then he looks up enquiringly.*)

SCHÖN (*wearily spelling it out*): P–E–R–S. . . .

The Spot fades out with circus music and applause.

SCENE THREE

Spot on LULU in front of mirrors Up Stage Right in a seductive black raincoat and with a tiny umbrella. She dances and strikes provocative poses to a storm of applause. She smiles and blows kisses. The applause dies as lights up on a theatre dressing room. Up Stage Centre a Spanish screen. Stage Left a door. Stage Centre, chairs and a table with costumes on it. Stage Right a dressing table and chair in front of a mirror.

ALWA is filling two glasses with wine. LULU runs in behind the screen to change.

ALWA: I've never seen an audience so enthusiastic.

LULU: Don't give me too much. Is your father here tonight?

ALWA: I don't know.

LULU: He doesn't want to see me. It's his fiancée.

ALWA: No he has business worries.

   SCHÖN *enters Left.*

We were just talking about you.

LULU (*popping her head over the screen*): You say in your papers I'm the most dazzling dancer on the stage and you're not even interested enough to come and see if you're right.

SCHÖN: Of course I'm right. It's almost impossible to get seats . . . You must learn to keep down stage more.

LULU: I have to get used to the lights.

SCHÖN (*to Alwa*): You don't show your dancers off to their best advantage. You don't understand enough about technique. (*to* LULU) What do you come on as next?

LULU: A flower girl.

SCHÖN (*to* ALWA): In tights?

ALWA: No, an ankle length dress. I'm only interested in a dancer's feet.

SCHÖN: It's not what the audience is interested in. Anyone with her looks doesn't need all your symbolic nonsense.

ALWA: The audience wasn't bored.

SCHÖN: Of course not. My newspapers have been telling them she's marvellous for the last six months. Was Prince Escerny here? I've arranged for him to come backstage.

ALWA: Nobody was here.

SCHÖN: Only you could let a dancer appear through two whole acts in a *raincoat*! (*He exits.*)

ALWA (*to* LULU): I don't want you upset by his rudeness.

   LULU *steps out from behind the screen in a period, sleeveless white dress.* ALWA *hands her a drink.*

LULU: If I'd sold flowers outside the Alhambra Café in this they'd have put me behind bars.

ALWA: You were only a child.

LULU (*drinking*): Do you remember when I came to your room for the first time?

ALWA: You wore a blue dress trimmed with black velvet.

LULU: Your father didn't know where to hide me.

ALWA: It's lucky mother was already bedridden.

LULU: You were playing with a toy theatre.

ALWA: Ah that toy theatre. In those days I thought of you as high above me, as high as the sun above the abyss. You were very worldly even then, but you asked me what 'Tristan and Isolde' was about.

LULU: I still don't know.

ALWA: I haven't forgotten the first time I kissed you.

LULU: I don't remember.

ALWA: When I found out why you were really in our home . . .

LULU: You changed.

ALWA: Just imagine, when mother died, I told my father that he must marry you immediately or I'd challenge him to a duel.

LULU: He told me.

ALWA: He'll never understand me. Now he thinks I'm working against his marriage to the von Zarnikov woman.

LULU: Is she still so naïve?

ALWA: She loves him. Her family wanted her to break off the engagement, but she insisted.

LULU: He only launched me in the theatre so I'd meet someone rich enough to marry me. I'm to dance my way into a millionaire's heart. And you're supposed to compose the music.

ALWA: You know I've always wanted to write a play for you. I'd give your role every mad improbability.

The bell rings over the door.

LULU: My scarf!

ALWA *puts it around her shoulders.*

LULU: I must remember to keep well down stage!

She exits Left. ALWA *sits at the table sipping his drink, and feeling the texture of the dresses from time to time.*

ALWA (*musing*): One could certainly write an interesting play about her . . . Act One Dr Goll . . . difficult . . . I'd have to conjure him back from the second circle of Hell and everybody'd blame me for his sins . . . (*Muffled sound of applause off Left.* ALWA *looks up*) . . . feeding time at the zoo . . . (*Returns to musing.*) Act Two Walter Schwarz . . . impossible . . . to see a man stripped naked and blasted by thunderbolts . . . Act Three? . . . Act Three . . . can it go on like this . . .?

PRINCE ESCERNY, *a blond, exquisitely dressed man, enters. Behaving as if he were at home he nods absently to* ALWA *and sits down at the dressing table. A silence. They listen to the sound of the audience off.*

ESCERNY: It's going well now.

ALWA: She's stretching her number again.

ESCERNEY: I had the pleasure of meeting her at your father's house. I've been negotiating with him about the publication of my articles on Lake Tanganyika.

ALWA: He's very interested in your work.

ESCERNY: When she dances she becomes intoxicated with her own beauty.

ALWA: I've planned it so she has six solo appearances, each one more daring than the last. But she'll dissipate the whole effect if she reveals too much of herself too soon. Here she is.

They both rise. ALWA *opens the door and* LULU *hurries in.*

LULU: I took three curtain calls.

ALWA (*gesturing*): Prince Escerny.

LULU: Isn't Herr Schön in your box. He must have left.

ESCERNY: He has the last box in the stalls on the left. I saw him clap.

LULU: Ah . . .

ALWA: Get a little rest if you can. (*He exits.*)

LULU: I must change.

ESCERNY: Your dresser isn't here.

LULU: I can do it quicker alone. I've still five more costume changes to make . . .

She steps behind the screen. ESCERNY *reacts with pleasure as she puts her underclothes on top of the screen. She throws her stocking over.* ESCERNY *furtively picks it up and starts playing with it.*

ESCERNY: Forgive me, but did I see you smile sadly when you took your bows? Am I right in believing that you suffer inwardly at having to degrade your art in front of people whose interest is, to say the least, of a dubious nature . . .?

26

(*He twists the stocking round his neck.*) Am I right in believing you'd exchange all this for a peaceful secluded existence? *Ugh* . . . (*He nearly strangles himself with the stocking.*) Am I also right in feeling you could keep a man at your feet and enjoy his utter helplessness.

ESCERNY *pockets the stocking as* LULU *steps out from behind the screen in a short pleated petticoat, white satin corset, white stockings and carrying white boots with spurs on the heels.* ESCERNY'S *walking stick jumps upright in his hand at the sight. His eyes continually go back to* LULU'S *glittering spurs. She crosses to the centre table and sits on it to put on her boots.*

LULU: If I miss just one evening I dream all night that I've been dancing. And next morning I wake up exhausted.

ESCERNY: But what a difference it would make if instead of dancing for that mob, you dance for an audience of one. (*He leans forward.*) A *chosen* one . . .

LULU: It'd make no difference to me. I don't see anybody when I'm dancing.

ESCERNY: You'd have a place worthy of you – a villa – a summer house – waves lapping on the shore. When I'm in Africa I have to exercise the most inhuman discipline.

LULU (*putting her foot up adjusting the spurs*): Africa's the place for it I'm told.

ESCERNY: Now I have a longing to surrender myself into a woman's power. It's a natural need to relax. Can you imagine any greater happiness for a woman than to have a man completely in her power? (*He bends down and spins her spurs.*)

LULU (*laughing*): Oh yes! (ESCERNY *flicks her spurs round quicker.*) Nobody's going to satisfy your desires without deceiving you at the same time.

ESCERNY (*spinning the spurs more furiously*): To be deceived by a woman like you, would be more rewarding than to be loved faithfully by an honest woman.

LULU: You've never been loved by an honest woman in your life!

LULU *kicks the delighted* ESCERNY *on to the floor. She slides off the table and crouches beside him.*

Undo this knot for me, please? I've laced myself up too tight. I get so excited when I dress.

    ESCERNY *tries to undo the corset knot, but his hands are trembling at the sight of the spurs.*

ESCERNY: I'm sorry . . .

LULU: I think I can do it.

ESCERNY (*elegantly wiping his brow*): I lack a certain dexterity with women's clothes.

LULU: You can't have had much opportunity to practise in Africa. (*loosening the knot*) I can breathe again.

    Trembling with pleasure ESCERNY *crawls to her to find himself between her thighs. She gets up and rests a foot on his back to do up her boot. He jerks sideways and she finds herself astride him.*

ESCERNY (*excitedly*): The thing that attracts me about you isn't your dancing . . . It's your physical – and spiritual – grace! I can see it in your dancing. You're generous, unselfish. You'd make any man happy and I know you could never deceive him, you're not a good enough actress!

    The bell rings. To ESCERNY'S *dismay she gets off him. But as a parting gesture she kicks him on the backside. He gasps with joy.*

ESCERNY: Oh . . .! May I stay a little longer?

LULU: Please do.

ESCERNY: I need to compose myself.

    LULU *exits.*

(*musing*) What is nobility? Is it a certain eccentricity as in my case. Or physical perfection as it is with that girl. (*Loud applause heard off Left.*) Wouldn't her children be more aristocratic than the children of some woman who had no more vitality than me . . .?

    ALWA *enters, catching* ESCERNY *still on the floor. He carries it off with aplomb stretching out elegantly.* ALWA *looks mildly surprised.* ESCERNY *rises gracefully.*

The audience seems most appreciative.

ALWA: I think white suits her best.

ESCERNY (*reflectively*): White makes her look too thin.

ALWA: You think so? White emphasizes her childish quality.

ESCERNY: I prefer pink. It brings out the woman

He takes out a handkerchief to wipe his brow, instead it is Lulu's stocking. ALWA *reacts. Shouts and great cries of alarm off Left.*

ALWA (*jumping up*): My God! There's been an accident! It's Lulu!

He rushes out followed by ESCERNY *Sounds of alarm off Left grow louder and louder. Finally* LULU *runs in half naked, and rushes behind the screen.*

ALWA hurries back in.

ALWA: You fainted?

LULU: Close the door.

ALWA: Come back on stage!

LULU: Did you see him with his fiancée?

ALWA: With his fiancée?

SCHÖN enters.

That's a joke you might have spared her!

SCHÖN (*locking the door*): What's wrong with her?

LULU: I feel I've been beaten all over.

SCHÖN: I'm responsible for you! You're going to dance!

LULU: In front of your fiancée?

SCHÖN: You'll dance in front of anyone who buys a ticket.

ALWA: If you'd only stayed in your box! (*to* LULU) Tell me what to do? (*knocking at the door*) . . . the Stage Manager . . . (*calling*) Just a minute . . ! Are you going to make us stop the performance?

SCHÖN: Get on stage.

LULU: Leave me alone. I feel ill.

ALWA: Damn all this backstage intrigue!

LULU: Put on the next number instead of me. No one will mind if I dance now or five minutes later.

ALWA: You will dance then?

LULU: As well as I can.

ALWA: As badly as you like, only dance. (*knocking again*) I'm coming.

He rushes out. There is the sound of the audience slow hand-clapping and stamping their feet. LULU *emerges from behind the screen in a flimsy black dressing-gown.*

LULU: You were right to put me in my place. And you couldn't have done it better than by letting me dance for your fiancée.

SCHÖN: Consider yourself lucky to have the chance to dance for decent people.

LULU: I don't care what anybody thinks of me. I don't want to be any better than I am.

SCHÖN: You're speaking the truth for once.

Waltz music heard off stage Left. Audience noise quietens down.

LULU (*off-handed*): The Prince was here.

SCHÖN (*turning to her*): Good. . . .

LULU: He's taking me to Africa.

SCHÖN: Africa?

LULU: Why shouldn't he? That's why you've made me a dancer, so somebody can carry me off.

SCHÖN: But not to *Africa*!

LULU: Why didn't you let me just faint.

SCHÖN: Because I didn't believe in your so-called fainting fit.

LULU (*closer to him*): The reason is you couldn't stand it down there with her any longer . . .

SCHÖN: No.

LULU (*softly*): Perhaps you were afraid I really hurt myself.

SCHÖN: I know you're indestructible.

LULU (*smiling*): You know that do you?

SCHÖN: Don't you smile at me.

LULU: Nobody's keeping you here.

SCHÖN: I'll go when the bell rings.

LULU: If you have the energy you mean. Where's all your energy gone? You've been engaged three years. Why don't you get married?

SCHÖN (*banging on the table with his stick*): It's *you*!

From now till the end of the scene, LULU *speaks and acts on a rising note of exultation.*

LULU: If you only knew how happy your rage makes me. You degrade me because you think you'll get over me quicker.

SCHÖN: I'm not afraid of you.

LULU: I don't want your fear. Go back to her. Don't put the blame on me. You have such faith in my integrity. You think

30

I'm a whore with a heart of gold. I'm neither one nor the other.

SCHÖN: I'll be married in eight days. Just keep away from me till then.

LULU (*smiling*): I'll lock my doors.

SCHÖN (*in sudden rage*): If you knew how I curse you!

LULU: All right I'll take all the blame. It's all my fault. Now you can feel pure, guiltless. You couldn't marry that sweet innocent otherwise could you?

SCHÖN (*clutching the air*): I'll kill you.

LULU: Yes, yes, what more do I have to say to make you?

SCHÖN: Stop talking! Stop talking!

LULU: Marry her and she'll dance in misery in front of me instead of me in front of her.

SCHÖN (*grabs her throat; splutters*): K-K-K . . .
  But instead of strangling her he kisses her savagely

LULU (*gasping*): Where's your whip? . . .
  SCHÖN *suddenly staggers back and rushes away to the door. About to wrench it open he stops, then straightens up slowly.*

SCHÖN: Can't face her like this . . . can't see people . . . must go home . . .

LULU (*gliding up to him, grabbing him*): Look at yourself for once. You always do exactly what you want and you know it.
  LULU *pushes him into a chair.*

LULU: You're too weak to tear yourself away from me. . . .

SCHÖN (*collapsing*): Ahhhhhhhh . . . (*Holds head in his hands.*)
  The music off stage Left stops. Now the audience is heard shouting and slow hand-clapping. Low at first, it grows in ferocity and volume throughout the rest of the scene.

LULU (*hugging herself*): Oh I'm happy . . . I'm happy . . .

SCHÖN: I'm an old man – the evening of my life.

LULU: The tyrant's crying. Go and tell your fiancée what kind of woman I am.

SCHÖN (*sobbing*): The sweet innocent . . .

LULU: You've gone soft. You've got nothing more for me. You can go to her now.

SCHÖN: I can't.

LULU: Outside. Come back when you're strong.

SCHÖN: What am I going to do?

LULU sweeps the cloths on the table on to the floor. There is some writing paper underneath. As she puts it in front of SCHÖN the baying crowd begins to chant 'Lulu . . . Lulu . . . Lulu . . .'

LULU: Write!

She stands erect behind his chair as she dictates the letter. The lights begin to go slowly down to a Spot on the two of them.

SCHÖN: I can't write . . . (*Picks up a pen.*)

LULU: My dear Countess von Zarnikov.

SCHÖN: I call her Adelaide.

LULU (*implacable*): My dear Countess von Zarnikov.

SCHON (*writing*): My death sentence . . .

LULU: 'You must take back your promise to marry me.'

SCHÖN (*writing*): Yes . . . Yes . . .

LULU: 'I am unworthy of your love . . .' (SCHÖN *hesitates, looks at her.*) Write, 'unworthy of your love'. (SCHÖN *writes. The crowd roars and chants.*) 'I have been trying to break away for three years. I haven't had the strength. I am at the side of the woman who rules me. Forget me. Herr Ludwig Schön.'

SCHÖN: Oh God!

LULU (*suddenly frightened*): Don't say that . . . (*regaining composure*) 'P.S. Do not try to save me'.

As he writes the crowd roars ferociously. LULU backs away into the darkness, leaving SCHÖN alone in the Spot. He stops writing and stares at the letter. The crowd seems to be breaking up the theatre: its savage roaring and chanting reaches a climax.

SCHÖN (*looking up*): Now comes the execution.

Wedding bells peal out above the crowd's roar which fades down immediately. Spot Up on LULU in front of the mirrors, dazzling in black underwear and a white bridal veil. SCHÖN'S Spot slowly out as he turns and sees her walk slowly Down Stage Right in front of the curving wall of mirrors as the Wedding March plays over.

The Wedding March continues over as LULU *stops Down Stage Right in front of the first mirror. Circus music up.* FERDINAND, *a bearded gamekeeper, enters with a white negligee. As* LULU *takes off the veil and* FERDINAND *helps her on with the negligee. Spot up Down Stage Left on* SCHÖN *watching them.*

FERDINAND *and* LULU *kiss.* SCHÖN *reacts violently.* FERDINAND *exits.* LULU *adjusts the negligee and finally turns away, smiling.*

Mirrors up. Music fades out. Lights up on a large room in German Renaissance style with heavily carved walls. At the rear of the room Up Stage a gallery leading to a staircase which sweeps down to the depth of half the stage, Stage Left. There is a door at the end of the gallery and a window halfway along it. Up Stage Centre under the gallery are the main doors. Down Stage Left, french windows behind curtains.

Stage Right a fireplace with a Chinese screen in front. Above it, LULU'S *portrait in an antique frame. Nearby, a curtained door to a small room. Down Stage Right a sofa. Stage Centre a table with heavy tablecloth and chairs.*

COUNTESS GESCHWITZ *is seated on the sofa watching* LULU. *She is dressed in a tight-waisted huzzar's jacket, high stiff collar, enormous cuff links, hands clasped inside a muff.*

GESCHWITZ (*to* LULU): I'm so looking forward to seeing you at the Ball.

SCHÖN: Isn't there a chance of a mere male being smuggled in?

GESCHWITZ: That'd be high treason Herr Schön. It's a Ball for women artists only.

SCHÖN (*indicating flowers on table*): What beautiful flowers.

LULU: The Countess Geschwitz brought them for me.

GESCHWITZ: You will be coming as a man, won't you?

LULU: Do you think it'll suit me?

    GESCHWITZ *gestures expressively to the portrait.*

My husband doesn't like it.

GESCHWITZ (*getting up and looking at the picture*): Is it by a local artist?

LULU: You wouldn't have known him.

GESCHWITZ: He's dead?

SCHÖN (*sotto*): He'd had enough.

LULU: You're in a bad mood today.

GESCHWITZ: I must go Madame Schön. I have so much to do for the Ball – Herr Schön.

    SCHÖN *and* GESCHWITZ *click their heels and bow formally.*
    LULU *escorts* GESCHWITZ *out Up Stage Centre.*

LULU: You'll stay to dinner tonight?

SCHÖN (*looking round shuddering*): It's the Aegean Stables. Filth. Her lover's everywhere. This is how I end my days. Filth. Thirty years hard work at the Stock Exchange and I finish up with . . . (*looking round*) There's somebody listening! (*He takes a gun from his breast pocket.*) They're *everywhere* . . . My life isn't safe. (*Holding the gun cocked he tiptoes to the french windows; listens a moment then rips open the curtains. There is nobody there.*) Filth! (*He walks back.*) I'm not mad. Men I can fight, but this . . . Filth . . . Filth . . . Filth . . .

    He hears LULU *coming and quickly pockets the gun.* LULU *enters.*

LULU: Couldn't you be free this afternoon? I'd like to ride in the park.

SCHÖN: You know I have to be at the Stock Exchange.

LULU: I'd rather be dead than let my life be ruined by money.

SCHÖN: He who takes life easily, dies easily.

LULU: I've always had a terrible fear of death.

SCHÖN: That's why I married you.

LULU (*crosses to him puts arm round his neck*): You didn't marry me.

SCHÖN (*stroking her hair*): Who did I marry then?

LULU: *I* married you.

SCHÖN: Does it make any difference?

LULU: I'm always afraid it may make a lot of difference.

SCHÖN: It's certainly changed a few things.

LULU: There's one thing it hasn't changed.

SCHÖN: What's that?

LULU (*sincerely*): Your love for me.

    SCHÖN *stumbles in surprise. They exit Up Stage Centre. As they do so* COUNTESS GESCHWITZ *enters through the curtains Stage Left. She comes warily into the room, and looking round sees* LULU'S *handkerchief in the chair. She picks it up and smells it. Hiding it in her muff she bends down at the sofa and smells where* LULU *has been sitting. As she does so there is a sound of voices. Panicking* GESCHWITZ *hides behind the firescreen.*

    SCHIGOLCH *enters by the gallery door, followed by* RODRIGO, *a strong man and acrobat, in a suit one size too small for him, and a fierce wax moustache. He is carrying a schoolboy,* HUGENBURG *under his arm.*

SCHIGOLCH: That fire escape'll be the death of me. Thank God we're home again.

HUGENBURG (*struggling in* RODRIGO'S *arms*): I'll be expelled from school!

RODRIGO: Your father's the Chief of Police, but you haven't the guts of a louse.

SCHIGOLCH (*slipping*): Some bloody idiot's waxed these stairs again.

HUGENBURG (*kicking his legs; wailing*): I'll be expelled from school! What do you mean by bringing me here?

RODRIGO: Think yourself damn lucky she saw you loafing in the Lantern Café and hired the old man and me to fetch you. It's not everyone has the chance of meeting the famous dancer Lulu and all you do is squeak – 'I'll be expelled from school – I'll be expelled from school.'

HUGENBURG: I will. I will.

RODRIGO: You're not even at a decent school yet.

SCHIGOLCH: There's been a few good lessons taught in this place, Master Hugenburg, so there's no need to be shy. But first a drop of the stuff money can't buy.

    Rubbing his hands he opens a small cupboard under the stairs and brings out a bottle and glasses.

RODRIGO: Alfred, you've been selected to attend one of Lulu's intimate afternoon soirées. (*He laughs.*) Only close friends like

the old man and me and young boys like yourself are invited.
But there's one thing I can promise, it'll be an afternoon you'll
remember!

HUGENBURG: If she doesn't dance in here pretty quick, I'll make
you wish you'd never been born!

RODRIGO: So you're going to beat up the strongest man in the
world, eh? (*He pulls an iron bar out of his pocket and bends it.*)
Get your father to give you long pants first.

HUGENBURG (*agitated*): If only I knew what to say to her.

RODRIGO (*sitting*): She'll know better than you.

SCHIGOLCH *puts the bottle and three glasses on the table and
starts pouring.*

SCHIGOLCH: I opened this 'un yesterday.

RODRIGO (*covering* HUGENBURG'S *glass*): Don't give him too
much or he won't be able to do himself justice and Lulu'll
make us suffer for it.

Joining them at the table HUGENBURG *takes out a cigar case
and hands it round.*

HUGENBURG (*importantly*): Imported Havannas.

RODRIGO *and* SCHIGOLCH *take one.*

RODRIGO: With the compliments of the Chief of Police.

SCHIGOLCH *and* RODRIGO *bite off the ends of their cigars.*
HUGENBURG *imitates them but bites his cigar in half by mistake.*

HUGENBURG: Do you live here with her?

RODRIGO: Of course we live here.

SCHIGOLCH: At home every Stock Exchange day when the
old man's out.

HUGENBURG: I wrote her a poem yesterday.

RODRIGO: What did you write her?

HUGENBURG: A poem.

RODRIGO (*to* SCHIGOLCH): A poem.

HUGENBURG (*bringing out a pile of papers*): Shall I read it to you?

SCHIGOLCH: What's he talking about?

RODRIGO: His poem. He wants to torture her a little first.

SCHIGOLCH *suddenly leans over the table and stares into*
HUGENBURG'S *eyes.*

SCHIGOLCH (*mocking*): His eyes. It's his eyes. His eyes.

RODRIGO: They've stopped her sleeping for the past week.

The two laugh and drink. LULU *enters Stage Centre in an elegant white ball gown with deep decolleté and flowers in her bosom.*

LULU: Quiet, children, I'm expecting a visitor.

HUGENBURG *has half risen, but* LULU *motions for him to remain seated.*

LULU: This is fine company you're keeping.

SCHIGOLCH: What's that you've got stuck out in front of you?

LULU: Orchids. Do you like them? (*Inclines her bosom over* HUGENBURG.) Smell. (HUGENBURG *nearly slides off the chair.*)

SCHIGOLCH: I'm going to find something to stick on me.

He picks a flower from those on the table and pins it on himself.

RODRIGO: Is Prince Escerny coming?

LULU: God forbid.

RODRIGO (*to* SCHIGOLCH): He wanted to marry her at one time.

SCHIGOLCH: I wanted to marry her at one time, too.

RODRIGO (*about to drink, his glass remains poised in mid air*): You wanted to marry her at one time?

SCHIGOLCH: Didn't you want to marry her at one time?

RODRIGO: Of course I wanted to marry her at one time.

SCHIGOLCH: Everybody wants to marry her at one time. But she never lets anybody regret they didn't marry her at one time.

RODRIGO: But isn't she your daughter?

SCHIGOLCH: It never crossed her mind.

HUGENBURG (*to* LULU *who is on top of him*): What's your father's name?

SCHIGOLCH: She never had one.

LULU: Of course I had one, I'm not a freak. (*to* HUGENBURG) Do you like your father?

RODRIGO: He should. He smokes a very decent cigar.

SCHIGOLCH: I suppose I should've locked the door in case he comes back unexpected.

RODRIGO: No need. He's at the Exchange.

LULU: But he's very suspicious. He's suffering from persecution mania.

RODRIGO *bounds up.*

RODRIGO: Don't worry, I'll deal with him. (*He lays back on the table, bent legs in the air.*) I'll put him on my feet then – alla-op! (*He jerks his legs up straight.*) He'll find himself plastered on the ceiling.

LULU: He'll scare you green with one of his looks.

RODRIGO: Scare *me*? (*Slaps his arms.*) Feel these muscles.

LULU (*crossing to him*): Let me see.

RODRIGO (*flexing them*): Granite . . .

LULU (*feeling them*): Mmmmm . . . If only you hadn't got such long ears.

FERDINAND, *the bearded gamekeeper in a grotesquely ill-fitting uniform, enters Stage Centre.*

FERDINAND (*announcing*): Herr Schön, Madam.

The three men react violently.

HUGENBURG: Eeeeeek!

RODRIGO: The bastard!

RODRIGO *dives across to the firescreen to hide behind it. He staggers back as the unseen* GESCHWITZ *moves it away.*

RODRIGO: Ahhh, *Jesus!*

HUGENBURG, *meanwhile, has slid straight off his chair and under the table. Wheezing painfully,* SCHIGOLCH *drags himself up the stairs to the gallery at a tottering gallop.* RODRIGO *attempts to dive under the table but* HUGENBURG *is already there.* FERDINAND *regards their frenzied reactions impassively.*

FERDINAND: Madam . . . ?

LULU: I'll receive him.

FERDINAND *exits.* RODRIGO *dives behind the curtained windows Stage Left.* HUGENBURG *looks out from under the table cloth.*

HUGENBURG (*whispering up to* LULU): Perhaps he won't stay . . . then we can be alone.

LULU *pushes him back with the tip of her toe: he kisses it and pops out of sight as* ALWA *enters in evening dress.*

ALWA: Matinees are getting later all the time . . . (*Notices* SCHIGOLCH *noisily dragging himself up the stairs.*) Who's that?

LULU: An old friend of your father's. They were in the war together.

ALWA (*eyes following* SCHIGOLCH): Is my father here then?

LULU: No. He had to go to the Exchange. We're going to have lunch together . . . (*the screen moves back into place; she distracts his attention*) How do you think I look?

ALWA: Don't ask me. I might say more than I should.

LULU: I mean my gown.

ALWA: Your dressmaker knows every curve of your body.

LULU: When I see myself in a mirror, I want to be a man. My own husband.

ALWA: I know. To enjoy the happiness you give him.

ALWA *looks at her with sly pleasure.* FERDINAND *thunders in with a trolley fuming with jealousy. He smiles at* LULU *and glares viciously at* ALWA *his beard trembling with rage. He plonks down the champagne bottle and throws the flowers away.*

ALWA (*to* FERDINAND): Have you got toothache?

LULU (*smiling*): Don't . . .

ALWA: Why are you so miserable?

FERDINAND (*through clenched teeth*): I'm only human . . .

Throwing all the cutlery on the table he clumps out. ALWA *and* LULU *sit opposite each other. Their actions grow increasingly frenzied.*

LULU: What I've always admired about you is your strength of character. You've always defended me like a brother.

ALWA: Please don't talk about it now. It's my . . .

A burb is heard from under the table. ALWA *frowns, puzzled, and is about to lift the table cloth.* LULU *stops him.*

LULU (*quickly*): That was me.

ALWA: You? . . . What was I saying? Oh yes . . . it's my fate to do good despite, dubious motives.

LULU:You always make yourself out to be so bad.

ALWA: Why are you flattering me like this?

LULU: You're the only man in the world who's defended me without degrading me.

ALWA: It hasn't been easy . . .

She opens the champagne, the cork shoots into the air. ALWA *grows more agitated. He lifts the table cloth.* HUGENBURG *pulls it down. When* ALWA *bends to look* LULU *pretends she has done it.*

ALWA: You make people criminals without realizing you're doing it. If we hadn't grown up as brother and sister . . .

He gets up and moves away. LULU *crosses to him.*

LULU: That's why you're the only man I can be open with.

ALWA: There are moments when I feel my soul collapse. The more discipline a man imposes on himself, the easier he goes to pieces. There's no . . .

He sees the table move. As he bends down to investigate LULU *interposes herself.*

LULU (*calmly*): What are you looking for?

ALWA: Nothing . . . You know you mean more to me than . . .

As he goes to embrace her HUGENBURG'S *hand creeps out and covers* LULU'S *breast.* ALWA'S *hand covers* HUGENBURG'S *thinking it is* LULU'S. FERDINAND *enters with a soup tureen and stares with fury.* ALWA *gets up embarrassed.* LULU *hits* HUGENBURG'S *hand away and joins* ALWA *at the table.*

ALWA: You look ill.

LULU: Leave him alone.

Raging FERDINAND *pours the soup straight from the tureen into the bowls.*

FERDINAND: I'm not used to waiting on table.

ALWA: You should see a doctor.

FERDINAND (*stirs the soup with gloved finger and flicks it into* ALWA'S *eye*): I'm the gamekeeper!

As he throws the tureen on to the table and storms out we see he has a dead rabbit hanging on the back of his belt. At that moment SCHÖN *enters by the gallery door and creeps forward silently.*

LULU: What were those moments when your soul collapsed?

ALWA (*up*): It's not something you talk about over lunch.

LULU: I've hurt you. (*She gives him her hand, he takes it and suddenly starts kissing it passionately.*) What are you doing?

RODRIGO sticks his head out of the curtains. LULU *gives him an angry look over* ALWA'S *shoulder.* RODRIGO *pops his head back not noticing that* SCHÖN *has let out a loud 'ahh!', pulled a gun and is coming determinedly down the stairs after him.*

ALWA (*clutching her hand*): Oh, this hand . . .

LULU: What's there to a hand?

ALWA: An arm and a body.

LULU: What's there to a body?

ALWA: Mignon! Mignon!

> *She snatches her hand from him, gets up and flings herself on to the sofa.*

ALWA (*kneeling beside her*): Destroy me!

LULU: Do you love me then?

ALWA: Do you love me, Mignon?

LULU: Love? Me? Nobody.

ALWA: I love you.

> *As he buries his head in her lap,* SCHÖN *reaches the curtains Stage Left.*

LULU (*softly*): I poisoned your mother . . .

> RODRIGO *sticks his head out of the curtains again, and comes face to face with the barrel of* SCHÖN'S *gun. He gestures wildly to* LULU *and* ALWA, *to get* SCHÖN *to aim at them.* SCHÖN *turns, sees them, and lets out a loud cry.* LULU *leaps back with a scream sending* ALWA *sprawling on the floor.*
>
> *They watch petrified as* SCHÖN *crosses grimly.*

SCHÖN: Alwa!

> ALWA *stands up as in a trance.*

SCHÖN: There's been another revolution in Paris.

ALWA: Paris . . . that's where I want to go. I want to go to Paris.

> SCHÖN *starts to push* ALWA *off.*

SCHÖN: They've gone berserk at the office. Nobody knows what to write . . . You'd better get down there . . .

> *They exit Up Stage Centre.* RODRIGO *bursts out from behind the curtain and tries to rush upstairs.* LULU *stops him.*

LULU: He'll have somebody waiting for you out there.

RODRIGO (*panic-stricken*): He'll shoot me.

LULU: He's coming.

RODRIGO: Jesus!

> *He frantically lifts the table cloth,* HUGENBURG *pops out.*

HUGENBURG (*punching his toes*): No room!

> *Yelping with pain,* RODRIGO *hops over to and hides behind the*

curtained door Stage Right. Gun in hand, SCHÖN *comes back, goes deliberately to the curtains, Stage Left, and throws them back.*

SCHÖN: Where's he gone?

LULU *points to the window in the middle of the gallery.*

LULU: He jumped. He's a professional acrobat.

SCHÖN: I couldn't have known that. (*Turns to face her.*) You scum!

LULU: Shut up and kill me!

SCHÖN: I've given you everything. All I asked for was the respect any servant would show me. Your credit's run out, madame.

LULU: My credit's good for years yet! (*crossing to him*) How do you like my new dress?

SCHÖN: Get away from me or I'll go mad and kill my own son. You're a disease. (*Thrusts the gun on her.*) Here's the cure! Do it yourself!

LULU *slumps on the sofa and stares at the gun, turning it over and over.*

LULU: You're so trusting.

SCHÖN: Because I'm not afraid of a whore. I'll guide your hand.

LULU *points the gun at him. He bends over her. They struggle. She fires a shot at the ceiling.* HUGENBURG *and* GESCHWITZ'S *heads appear for a second and* RODRIGO *leaps out from behind the curtains, races up the stairs and dives straight through the gallery window as* LULU *leaps on* SCHÖN.

SCHÖN: What was . . .

LULU: Nothing. You're suffering from persecution mania.

SCHÖN: How many more lovers have you got hidden? (*Snatches the gun from her.*) Where are they?

He rushes to the french windows, and looks behind the curtain. GESCHWITZ *tries to creep away. With a yell of triumph he sees her and grabs her by the collar.*

GESCHWITZ: *ArrrrrrrrK!!!*

SCHÖN (*shaking her*): Are you an acrobat too? What did you do – come down the chimney?

GESCHWITZ: You're hurting me.

SCHÖN: Now you'll just have to stay to dinner.

GESCHWITZ: I'm not hungry.

He pushes her through the door Stage Right and then thrusts the gun at LULU *again.*

SCHÖN: Look at me! I'm not going to be cuckolded by my own son. Look at me!

LULU: Order the carriage. We'll drive to the opera.

SCHÖN: We'll drive to Hell. (*Turns the gun in* LULU'S *hand to her breast.*) Let it all come out. I don't care what happens now. Just so long as I rid the world of you. Finish it off. *Fire.*

LULU (*reasonably*): Divorce me.

SCHÖN: That's the last straw! And see you trample on my son too? The boy's longing for you. (*Reaches for the gun.*) Give it to me.

They struggle, she wrenches herself from him with the gun.

LULU: You know why you married me, and I know why I married you. You say you've sacrificed the evening of your life for me. But I've sacrificed my youth! I'm not sixteen any more but I'm still too young to die.

SCHÖN (*rushing at her*): Down murderess! On your knees, murderess! (*He forces her back.*) DOWN! (LULU *sinks to her knees.*) God give you strength to do it, murderess down!

HUGENBURG *suddenly leaps out from under the table, knocking a chair over and blubbering with fright.* SCHÖN *whirls round in surprise presenting his back to* LULU. *She rises and fires five shots into* SCHÖN *and continues pulling the trigger.* SCHÖN *staggers forward.* HUGENBURG *catches him.*

SCHÖN (*staring at* HUGENBURG): Another one of them.

LULU (*rushing to him*): Oh, God!

SCHÖN: Alwa!

LULU (*crying*): You're the only man I ever loved.

SCHÖN: Whore! Alwa! Alwa! Water . . .

LULU: Quick he's dying of thirst.

HUGENBURG *lets* SCHÖN *go and he crashes on to the floor.* LULU *pours him a glass of champagne and holds it to his lips.* ALWA *rushes in Stage Centre.*

I shot him.

HUGENBURG: She's innocent.

SCHÖN (*to* ALWA): You're the winner.

ALWA (*trying to lift him*): Get him to a bed . . .

SCHÖN (*screaming with pain*): Yeeeeeee . . . I'm burning . . .
(LULU *gives him another glass of champagne.*) Still true to type . . .
(*He drinks: to* ALWA) Don't let her escape.

ALWA (*to* HUGENBURG): Help me carry . . .

SCHÖN: More champagne . . .! More champagne . . .! More
champagne . . .!

> As HUGENBURG *and* ALWA *carry* SCHÖN *to the door Right,*
> GESCHWITZ *walks out.* SCHÖN *shudders, pushes the other two*
> *aside and draws stiffly up to his full height.*
> (*scornfully*) Another one of them . . . Madam!
> *He starts to bow and continues as he keels over dead. Wailing,*
> LULU *throws herself down beside him and kisses his face.*

LULU: It's over.

GESCHWITZ: Thank God, I thought he'd shot you.

> LULU *gets up and goes toward the stairs.*

ALWA: Stay where you are!

LULU (*throwing herself at* ALWA'S *feet*): Don't hand me over to
the police. I never loved anybody like I loved him. I'll do
anything you ask. I'll be faithful to you all my life Alwa, Alwa.
I'll belong to you always. Look at me, Alwa. Look at me.
Look at me.

> *Lights dim as loud knocking is heard from outside.*

ALWA: It's the police!

> *Two searchlights play around the room as* HUGENBURG *rushes*
> *panic-stricken up the gallery yelling and clutching the front of his*
> *trousers.*

HUGENBURG: I'll be expelled from school! I'll be expelled from
school. I'll be expelled . . .!

Lights out as circus music plays loudly over.

CURTAIN

ACT TWO

SCENE ONE

An unseen Judge raps three times for silence. A bell tolls mournfully. Distorted circus music is played at a very slow speed.

Spot up Up Stage Centre on a monstrous swaying image of LULU *in a fairground distorting mirror dressed in a prison smock and behind bars.*

Music fades down and LULU'S *spot is snapped off.*

Lights up on the same large drawing room as previous scene, only the furniture is covered in dust sheets. The curtains are drawn. The oil lamp on the table gives a soft glow. ALWA *paces the room, while* RODRIGO, *dressed as a footman, poses and flexes his muscles. Pale-faced and ill,* GESCHWITZ *dressed in black, sits huddled in an armchair, her legs covered with rugs.*

RODRIGO: Why's he keeping us waiting like this?

GESCHWITZ: Be quiet.

RODRIGO: How can I keep quiet when my brain is teeming with ideas? How does she look?

GESCHWITZ: Lovelier than ever.

RODRIGO: God help me if I have to rely on your tastes. If the cholera's left my Lulu looking like you then I'm bankrupt.

GESCHWITZ: What would be enough to kill the rest of us only increases her beauty.

RODRIGO (*determined*): I've made up my mind. I'm not going over the frontier with you this evening.

GESCHWITZ: You're going to let your bride travel alone?

RODRIGO: The old boy's going with her. If I went too they'd only get suspicious. Anyway I've got to stay here till my stage costumes are ready. I can get across the frontier later. She'll have to put a bit of flesh on her by that time. I'll only marry her if she can appear in front of a paying audience. I like a woman to be useful. Don't you agree Herr Schön?

45

ALWA: What did you say?

RODRIGO: I'd never got involved in all this if she hadn't thrown herself at me before the trial.

ALWA: I've been wondering if someone sentenced to penal servitude would make a suitable tragic figure for a modern drama.

GESCHWITZ: Where is he?

RODRIGO: I've still got to get my equipment out of hock: the finest pair of dumb-bells in Germany: 600 kilos of the best iron. You know, when I staggered into the pawnshop with them – dripping with sweat – that damn pawnbroker asked me if they were *real* . . . I'd have done better to have my stage costumes made abroad. (*He mimes the costumes.*) Paris tailors know how to bring out a man's good points. Here they're afraid of bare skin. Two years ago I was fined 50 marks at the Alhambra Theatre for showing a few hairs on my chest – not enough to make a decent toothbrush. (*He laughs.*) The Minister thought I'd make the young girls lose interest in their sewing. I've had to shave my chest every week since.

ALWA (*thoughtfully*): The curse of literature today is it's too literary. To bring about a re-birth in our art, we must show men and women who've never read a book. In my play *Earth Spirit* I tried to work on these principles. The woman I took as a model for the central character has been in prison for a year. As long as my father was alive, my plays could be performed in Germany. Now . . .

RODRIGO: I've had my tights made in the most delicate shade of grey-green. They're so beautifully cut I can't sit down. They show off my body marvellous – if I didn't have this damned pot-belly (*slaps stomach*) which I got being involved in your stupid schemes. Anyone'd get fat laying around in a hospital for three months. Ever since I came out, I've been stuffing laxatives down my gullet. By the time I get across the frontier, I'll be so weak I won't be able to lift a bottle let alone a pair of dumb-bells.

GESCHWITZ: In hospital yesterday the way the prison warders avoided her was wonderful.

46

RODRIGO: When I spread the word Sister Theophila here had cholera, you couldn't keep anyone in their beds.

ALWA (*crossing to* GESCHWITZ): Countess, Lulu shot my father, but I can't see the murder or the punishment as anything but shocking bad luck. I even believe my father wouldn't have disowned her, had he lived. I can't find the words to express my admiration for your sacrifice. Your superhuman contempt for death. I don't know how rich you are Countess but the expenses involved in this plan must have been considerable. May I again offer you the loan of 20,000 marks?

GESCHWITZ (*waving the offer aside*): Thank you no . . . What a strain it's been for my darling. I did her hair exactly like mine and imitated every inflection of her voice.

RODRIGO (*crossing to* ALWA): Now wait a minute! I had expenses too! I was in that hospital three months checking the routine and I've been a footman here so there'll be no strange servants in the house! I've had expenses too! . . .

Noises off.

SCHIGOLCH (*off*): That damn fire escape.

GESCHWITZ (*half rises, excitedly*): Here he comes.

SCHIGOLCH *enters from the gallery in a long black frock-coat and cane.*

SCHIGOLCH: Damn this darkness. The sun's scorching outside.

GESCHWITZ *is feebly disentangling herself from the rugs.*

RODRIGO: It's like living in a coffin. Have you fixed up where you're going to stay tomorrow?

SCHIGOLCH: Wherever it is, let's hope it isn't at Government expense.

RODRIGO: I can recommend a good hotel across the border. I lived there once with a lady lion-tamer.

GESCHWITZ (*still struggling up*): Help me, please. He's not going through with it.

ALWA *helps her.*

SCHIGOLCH (*sneering*): What you got, chilblains?

RODRIGO (*with dignity*): I'm waiting for my stage costumes. Anyway it won't do her any harm to be on her own a little at first.

47

GESCHWITZ: We don't need him. We'll rescue her alone.

GESCHWITZ supports herself by holding on to the back of a chair. ALWA *takes out a bundle of notes.*

ALWA: Here's 10,000 marks.

GESCHWITZ: Thank you, no . . . (*She moves up to the gallery: to* SCHIGOLCH) *Hurry.*

SCHIGOLCH: Patience, my dear, it's only a step to the hospital. We'll have her back here in five minutes.

ALWA: You're bringing her here?

RODRIGO (*sprawling in an armchair*): It's quite safe. According to the latest newspaper reports Herr Alwa Schön is on his way to Constantinople where his play *Earth Spirit* is being performed for the Sultan of Turkey . . . (*chuckles*) by naked concubines and eunuchs.

Leaning on SCHIGOLCH, GESCHWITZ *exits by the gallery door.* Why do you want to give that crazy old hag money?

ALWA: What's it got to do with you?

RODRIGO: 'Cause I'm penniless. And I had to bribe every single nurse in that hospital, the doctors too.

ALWA: Do you seriously expect me to believe that doctors allowed themselves to be bribed by you?

RODRIGO: In America I could make myself President with the money those men cost me.

ALWA: The Countess Geschwitz paid you back every penny. And you receive a monthly salary of 500 marks from her. It's sometimes hard to believe in your love for that unfortunate murderess . . . Actually I'm not altogether clear what claims you think you have on me. The mere fact you almost happened to see my father's murder doesn't automatically make us friends. I'm sure if Countess Geschwitz hadn't turned up, you'd be lying dead drunk in some gutter by now.

RODRIGO (*jumping up*): And where would you be if you hadn't sold your father's paper for two million? Living with some broken-down ballet dancer. What work do you do, eh? Wrote some damn play with my fiancée's legs as the two main characters. You worm! Why a year ago I was balancing two cavalry horses on my chest -- *saddled*! I don't know how I'm

48

going to get on now, with this belly. I can just see myself sweating through my tights every time I try lifting another kilo. A fine advertisement for German artistry . . .

ALWA: You spineless weakling.

RODRIGO: Are you trying to insult me? Listen, I'll make your tongue jump out your mouth and up the wall.

ALWA: You just try.

Voices and footsteps off.

ALWA: Who's that?

RODRIGO (*hastily smoothing his hair*): It's my beloved.

ALWA: No they can't be back so soon.

RODRIGO *looks alarmed.*

ALWA: Hide yourself. (*Indicates curtained windows.*)

RODRIGO: It's all right I know the way.

He hides behind the curtains as HUGENBURG *enters quickly by the gallery. He has changed; his hair is cropped and he is smoking a cigarette.*

ALWA: Aren't you . . .?

HUGENBURG (*furtively looking around*): Alfred Hugenburg I've got a plan. Can anyone hear us? This is foolproof. All I need is money to . . .

ALWA: What are you talking about?

HUGENBURG: I can rely on you. The evidence you gave at the trial helped her more than anything else. You were the defence's best witness.

ALWA (*recognizing him*): You're the boy who testified my father tried to force her to shoot herself.

HUGENBURG: So he did. But nobody believed me.

ALWA: Where've you come from?

HUGENBURG *pours himself a drink at the table.*

HUGENBURG: The reformatory. I broke out this morning. I'm hiding with a girl who's just had my father's bastard.

ALWA: Your father?

HUGENBURG: The Chief of Police. I know that prison, though I haven't been inside it, yet. None of the warders will recognize me. Not that I'm relying on that – oh no. There's an iron ladder in the front courtyard, I'll climb up to the roof and drop into the loft, there's piles of wood shavings there and I'll set light to them, I've got all the stuff and . . .

ALWA: But you'll be burnt to death.

HUGENBURG: Naturally if I'm not rescued. Now to get into the front courtyard I must have the warder on my side. I need money for that – not to bribe him, that wouldn't work. No, this is the clever part; I'll lend him the money to send his three children away for a holiday in the country. He'll be grateful and I'll be able to slip into the courtyard in the morning. By the afternoon the loft'll be blazing . . .

ALWA: How did you get out of the reformatory?

HUGENBURG: Jumped through a window . . .

 RODRIGO *steps from behind the curtain.*

RODRIGO: Shall I serve coffee here or on the verandah your lordship?

 HUGENBURG *lets out a cry and drops his glass.*

HUGENBURG: He came out of the same place last time!

ALWA: He's my footman now. He's quite dependable.

HUGENBURG (*clutching his head*): What a fool I am.

RODRIGO (*sarcastically*): 'Dropping into the loft . . . wood shavings . . . fire . . .' Don't you know the woman's dead? Cholera . . .

HUGENBURG: It's not true.

RODRIGO (*takes newspaper from his back pocket*): Here, read this.

HUGENBURG (*reading newspaper*): 'The murderess of Herr Ludwig Schön mysteriously contracted cholera in prison' . . . It doesn't say she's dead.

RODRIGO: In her grave these last three weeks. The far corner behind the rubbish dump. And after you've paid your respects – back to the reformatory or I'll hand you over to the police. (*grinning*) I happen to know that girl you're living with.

HUGENBURG (*to* ALWA): Lulu – dead?

ALWA: Yes, thank God.

HUGENBURG (*softly*): I'd have given anything . . . oh well I suppose I'll go to the devil one way or the other . . .

RODRIGO: How dare you bother Herr Schön and me. Bloody

little arsonist! (*grabs him by the scruff of the neck and propels him up the gallery*) Ten years hard is what you need to teach you not to meddle.

HUGENBURG (*wailing*): What a fool I am ... what ... Ahhhhh.
RODRIGO *boots him out of the gallery door.*

RODRIGO: And stay out! (*Comes back.*) I'm surprised you didn't hand over all your cash to that lout.

ALWA: He's got more courage in his little finger than you have in your whole body.

RODRIGO: I'm going to make my wife a wonderful trapeze artiste and I don't mind risking my life for it. But I'm going to be master in my own home. I'm going to have some say in the kind of lovers she has.

ALWA: That boy restores one's faith in youth. Do you remember how he leapt up at the trial and shouted, 'How would you've turned out if you'd danced barefoot as a child for pennies.'

RODRIGO: I could have bashed his face in. Thank God we have prisons to teach ruffians like that some respect for law and order. (*Sits, waxing his moustache.*) I've ordered a two-inch-thick bull whip. If that doesn't do the trick with her, I give up ... I'm going to rent a fifty-foot-high garage so I can train her properly. If she brings off her first double somersault without breaking her neck, I'm made. I won't need to lift a finger for the rest of my life. It's not half as much effort for a woman to keep a man as the other way round. It works out fine so long as the man takes care of the intellectual side and sees that a sense of the family doesn't go down the drain. I'll have to get her wages from the managers with a meat axe. I know that crowd of leeches ...

Dragging footsteps are heard in the gallery off. ALWA *tenses and turns.* RODRIGO *looks up.*

RODRIGO (*gesturing grandly*): Here she is – the most beautiful trapeze artiste of our time.

LULU *enters by the gallery door supporting herself on* SCHIGOLCH'S *arm. She is thin, white-faced and wearing the same black dress as* GESCHWITZ.

RODRIGO (*appalled*): Great Judas!

LULU (*coming down stairs*): Gently, you're hurting my arm.

RODRIGO: You've got the nerve to break out of jail looking like *that*!

SCHIGOLCH: Shut up!

RODRIGO: I've been robbed. I'll go to the police. I'll denounce the lot of you. This hag couldn't be seen anywhere in tights. I've been tricked.

ALWA: You vulgarian.

RODRIGO: Vulgarian! You realize I've got completely out of condition on account of this bag of bones. I've gone flabby. I'm unemployable thanks to you! *Swindlers!* I'm off to the police! (*He storms out by the gallery.*)

LULU: Don't worry, he wouldn't dare.

SCHIGOLCH: Good riddance.

LULU sits with a sigh.

LULU: Freedom . . .

SCHIGOLCH: I still have to buy the tickets for the sleepers. I'll come back for you in half an hour. We can celebrate your escape in the station buffet. I'll order a meal you'll remember . . .

He exits by the gallery. LULU seems to grow stronger immediately. She moves round pulling the dust covers off the furniture.

LULU: I haven't seen a room for eighteen months . . . curtains . . . armchairs . . . (*She sinks exhausted.*)

ALWA: Champagne?

LULU (*nodding*): It's just like old times. Where's my picture?

ALWA pours two glasses and brings them over to her.

ALWA: You haven't lost your vanity even in prison.

LULU: I was so frightened when I couldn't see myself. One day I got a new dustpan and I used to hold the underside to my face. The reflection wasn't very flattering but it made me feel fine. (*eagerly*) Let me see it.

ALWA crosses to the picture on the wall Right and pulls off the dust cover. LULU stares up at herself as Pierrot.

LULU: Did you look at it while I was away?

ALWA: No. I've been so busy selling the paper. Geschwitz

wanted to hang it in her house but she knew the police might come.

LULU: Now the poor monster is enjoying Government hospitality.

ALWA: What actually happened?

LULU: She arranged it very well. She went out of her way to contract cholera then she visited me in prison and gave it to me.

ALWA: Heroic!

LULU: We both finished up in the isolation wing of the hospital. Geschwitz was discharged yesterday.

ALWA: I know, she's been staying here.

LULU: She did all she could to make herself look like me. She came back just now and we exchanged places. I walked out free and she's lying there as the murderess of Herr Schön.

ALWA: That woman has the most extraordinary courage.

LULU: I'm a little thin in the face but otherwise I haven't changed have I?

ALWA: No.

LULU: What have you been doing in the last year and a half?

ALWA: I've had a certain success with a play I wrote about you.

LULU: Who's your mistress?

ALWA: An actress, I haven't seen her in six weeks.

LULU (*shuddering*): How can you stand that?

ALWA: I find there's a strange reciprocal action between sensuality and artistic creation. With you for example, I can either exploit you creatively or love you.

LULU (*falling on to the sofa, musing*): Every night in the prison I used to dream I'd fallen into the hands of a sex maniac . . . ahhhhh . . . (*She sits up.*) Kiss me.

ALWA (*kisses her*): Your lips have gone rather thin (*she pulls him down on the sofa*).

LULU: Do I disgust you? We only had a bath every four weeks. (*She kisses him passionately*.) I suppose you couldn't exploit me creatively now. (*stretching out her legs*) The only thing that really annoyed me was the ghastly shoes they made us wear.

Do you remember the fancy dress ball when I went as a man? All the women ran after me. Geschwitz crawled round my feet begging me to kick her in the face . . .

ALWA presses down to kiss her.

(*soothingly*) Shhh . . . I shot your father . . .

ALWA: I don't love you any the less for that.

She pushes his head back and kisses him.

You play with me like an expert. You're the most designing bitch . . .

LULU (*sincerely*): I only wish I were. (*kissing*) Come with me to Paris. Come with me. We'll change our names. And just be happy together.

ALWA: Yes . . .

They kiss passionately; LULU *looks round.*

LULU: Isn't this the sofa your father bled to death on?

ALWA: Be quiet . . . be quiet . . .

They continue kissing as lights dim down and out and discordant circus music is played over.

SCENE TWO

Spots up on the distorting mirrors. Only the centre panel is dark. Men and women in death masks waltz in front of them. RODRIGO *dances with* LUDMILLA STEINHERZ *dressed in a garish red and white striped frock.* ALWA *partners* BIANETTA *in a dark green velvet blouse and skirt studded with imitation topazes. Banker* PUNTSCHU *partners* MAGELONE *in a rainbow coloured dress of silk, the crippled journalist* HEILMAN *partners* MAGELONE'S *twelve-year-old daughter,* KADIDJA, *whilst* GESCHWITZ *in black dances alone. Their grotesquely distorted images form a moving Dance of Death fresco.*

The centre mirror lights to reveal LULU *in a white Directoire gown, long white kid gloves, hair high with a small plume of white feathers, dancing with the bejewelled* MARQUIS CASTI-PIANI, *a tall saturnine man with a bald head, black lips and painted fingernails. Lights up to show* LULU *and* CASTI-PIANI *and the others in a*

54

spacious drawing room with tall mirrors everywhere. Up Stage Centre are double doors half open to the gaming room beyond. Stage Left is a door to the dining room. Nearby LULU'S *picture as Pierrot. Stage Right, a door to the corridor. Near it, a small sideboard with a cold buffet. Stage Centre a love-seat.*

A fanfare and they remove their masks to a babble of conversation. RODRIGO *who is standing Stage Centre slightly drunk and uncomfortable in evening dress raises his glass in a toast.*

RODRIGO: Ladies and Gents . . . pardon me . . . quiet . . . I drink . . . Yes permit me to drink to the birthday . . . (*tearful*) yes the birthday of our gracious hostess . . . (*takes* LULU'S *arm*) Countess Adelaide d'Oubre . . . dammit! I say dammit . . . and so on . . . and so on . . .

ALL: The Count and Countess d'Oubre!

They all crowd round LULU *and* ALWA.

RODRIGO (*feeling his collar*): I'm sweating like a pig.

ALWA (*to* LULU): Let's see how things are doing at the tables.

They exit Up Stage.

BIANETTA (*to* RODRIGO): They tell me you're the strongest man in the world.

RODRIGO: And so I am, Miss. (*leering*) If you say yes, I'll have the pleasure of proving it to you.

BIANETTA: Personally I prefer sharp-shooters. Three months ago there was a sharp-shooter at the Casino; every time he went, '*bang*' '*bang*' I went, 'whroom' ' whroom'. (*She throws out her hips.*)

CASTI-PIANI (*to* MAGELONE): Tell me my dear, why are we having the honour of seeing your enchanting daughter for the first time tonight?

MAGELONE: Do you really think she's enchanting? She's still at the convent. She goes back to school Monday.

KADIDJA: What did you say, Mother?

MAGELONE: I was telling the gentleman you were top in geometry.

HEILMAN: What lovely hair she's got.

CASTI-PIANI: And her feet. The way she carries herself.

PUNTSCHU: She's got *breeding*.

MAGELONE: Come, come, gentlemen. She's just a child.

PUNTSCHU: That wouldn't trouble me. I'd give ten years of my life to get to know that little lady.

MAGELONE: Never, there's not enough money in the world. She's not going to be corrupted as I was.

CASTI-PIANI: The true confessions of a lady of virtue. Would you give your consent for say, a cluster of diamonds?

MAGELONE: Don't brag! There's no chance of you giving diamonds to my daughter or me either.

> MAGELONE *gestures to* KADIDJA *and she goes into the gaming room.*

GESCHWITZ: Isn't anyone going to play this evening?

LUDMILLA: But of course, Countess!

> CASTI-PIANI *offers his arm to* BIANETTA *and* LUDMILLA.

CASTI-PIANI: Ladies . . .

> *They exit into the gambling room, laughing.* PUNTSCHU *has seated himself heavily on the love-seat.*

MAGELONE: Have you any more Virgin shares for me, Herr Puntschu?

PUNTSCHU: Virgin shares? You mean Virgin Island shares. One must be exact in these matters, to avoid misunderstanding. I still have four thousand but I want to keep them.

HEILMAN: I keep telling my readers to buy, buy, buy. Virgins are always safe. I'm even taking my own advice. I'd like as many Virgins as I can get my hands on.

PUNTSCHU: I'll see what I can do. But you'll have to pay a stiff price for them! (*Roars with laughter.*)

MAGELONE: My fortune teller told me to buy Virgins. Everything I have is in those shares. If anything goes wrong . . .

PUNTSCHU: Trust me, my sweet.

ALWA (*returning from the gaming room: to* MAGELONE): I shouldn't worry. I paid a lot for my Virgins and I haven't regretted it, the price goes up every day.

MAGELONE (*pulling* PUNTSCHU *up*): Let's try our luck at baccarat.

They all go into the gaming room, leaving RODRIGO *and* GESCHWITZ *alone.* RODRIGO *who has been scribbling a note, looks up.*

RODRIGO: Ah, her ladyship. (GESCHWITZ *starts back: with attempted jocularity.*) Do I really look as dangerous as all that? (*low to himself*) I'll try a little 'bon mot' . . . (*mincing over to her smiling*) If I may be so bold . . .

GESCHWITZ (*snarling*): Go to Hell!

CASTI-PIANI *escorts* LULU *back into the room.*

CASTI-PIANI: A word with you.

As LULU *nods,* RODRIGO *surreptitiously passes her his note.*

RODRIGO (*bowing*): Countess d'Oubre, Monsieur Casti-Piani, I have the honour to excuse myself.

He exits knocking into a door-post.

CASTI-PIANI (*to* GESCHWITZ): Leave us alone, please.

LULU (*to* CASTI-PIANI): I've upset you again?

CASTI-PIANI (*to* GESCHWITZ *who hasn't stirred*): Are you deaf?

With a deep sigh GESCHWITZ *goes into the gaming room.* CASTI-PIANI *closes the door behind her.*

LULU: How much do you want this time?

CASTI-PIANI: You're broke. You gave me your last penny yesterday.

LULU (*shrugging*): If you say so.

CASTI-PIANI: You're high and dry, you and this writer.

LULU: Why all the talk. If you want me for yourself you don't have to use threats.

CASTI-PIANI (*going to sideboard picking up some hors d'oeuvre*): I know that, my dear child. I've had you to myself for six long months. But you must realize I haven't taken all your money because I loved you, but I loved you in order to take all your money. Actually I find Bianetta more attractive. You display the choicest cuts in front of a man, but after he's eaten, he finds himself hungrier than ever. All you do for a lover is ruin his digestion. And frankly you've loved too much, too long, even by our local standards. (*Comes back with a small plate of hors d'oeuvres.*) But that makes you very well qualified for the position I have in mind.

LULU: I haven't asked you for a job.

CASTI-PIANI: I told you I was an employment agent.

LULU (*taking asparagus from his plate*): You told me you were a police spy.

CASTI-PIANI: Only part time. Originally I was an employment agent till I slipped up over a clergyman's daughter. I 'procured' her a job in Valparaiso but the establishment there didn't come up to her expectations. She complained to her papa and I was clapped in prison. (*Eats delicately.*) But my exemplary character soon won the confidence of the police. They found they had to triple the police force on account of the recent bomb outrages and so they sent me here to Paris on an allowance of 150 marks a month. But who can live on 150 a month? So unlike most of my colleagues who have to be kept by women, I just resumed my former profession. I've been doing quite well. There's a goodly number of women with a hunger for life who I've managed to despatch to places where they can exercise their natural vocations.

LULU: I'd be no good at that.

CASTI-PIANI (*nibbling an olive*): I'm not interested in your opinion. The public prosecutor's paying 1,000 marks to anyone who hands over the murderess of Herr Ludwig Schön. 1,000 marks. On the other hand, the Oikonomopoulos Establishment in Cairo is offering £60 for you – that's 1,200 marks – 200 more than the public prosecutor. But naturally that's incidental, I want to see my mistresses happy.

LULU: I could never be happy in a brothel. Maybe when I was fifteen. Then I was so miserable I bought a gun to shoot myself. I was in hospital for three months. I never saw a man all that time but I saw myself. I used to dream of the man who was created for me. Since then I can tell in pitch darkness, at a range of a hundred feet, upwind, if a man's for me or not. If he isn't and I go with him, I feel sordid next day. I'm not giving myself to any Tom, Dick or Harry!

CASTI-PIANI: You won't find any Toms, Dicks, or even Harrys, at Oikonomopoulos of Cairo. His clientele is made up solely of Scottish Dukes, Russian dignitaries, Indian Princes and naturally, our own Rhineland Industrialists. You'll live in a princely apartment overlooking the minarets of the El-Azhar Mosque, stroll all day over Persian carpets eight inches deep, fabulous Parisian ball-room gowns, champagne on tap – and you'll even be your own mistress, up to a point. If you don't fancy a man you don't have to show any feelings for him. That's only fair, otherwise the whole thing would be impossible.

LULU: You don't expect me to believe your Egyptian friend will pay 500 francs for a woman he's never seen.

CASTI-PIANI: I took the liberty of sending him your pictures.

LULU: You sent the pictures I gave you?

CASTI-PIANI: I thought he'd appreciate them better than me. And there's another thing. You'll be safer with Oikonomopoulos in Cairo than anywhere else in the world. The German authorities would never extradite an Egyptian courtesan. It'd be too complicated and expensive.

LULU: Why don't you just ask me for the 1,200 marks if you need money.

CASTI-PIANI: You haven't got any money.

LULU: We have 30,000.

CASTI-PIANI (wiping his hands on a napkin): In shares. I never touch shares. The police pay me in good German marks, Oikonomopoulos in English gold. You could be on board by tomorrow. In fourteen days you'll be safe. You know as a member of the secret police myself it beats me how you've been able to live here a whole year without being discovered. There's something wrong with the whole system. But if I found out your past history, there's nothing to stop one of my colleagues getting on to you, especially in view of your heavy turnover in men. (Takes out a watch.) The train leaves at 12.30 tonight. If we haven't come to terms by eleven, I'll call the police. (Puts watch away.) I'm only concerned with your safety.

LULU: I'll go to America with you – China – anywhere. But I won't sell myself. That's worse than prison.

CASTI-PIANI takes out a letter from his pocket.

CASTI-PIANI: I'd like you to see this . . . (*Shows her the envelope and letter.*) Notice the Cairo postmark? Just in case you think I've forged it. The girl who wrote it is a Berliner. She was married to a former colleague of mine for two years. Now he's a foreign traveller for some company in Hamburg.

LULU: He probably visits her when he's in Cairo!

CASTI-PIANI: It's possible. Now listen to what she says. I don't think all that highly of my profession, but a cry of joy like this letter allows me a certain moral justification. (*He screws a monocle into his right eye, clears his throat.*) 'Dear Mr Meier' – Meier's the name I use when I'm shipping out the girls – 'Dear Mr Meier. When you're in Berlin go to the Conservatory in Postdamer Platz and ask for Gusti Von Rosenkron – she's the most beautiful woman I have ever seen – just how you like them. I have already written to her. She is twenty-two, no money and no prospects and pining for love. I've already spoken to the Madame here. Another German girl would be welcome, provided she's respectable. Italian and French girls can't compete with us Germans as they are very badly educated. If you see Fritz' – Fritz was her husband – 'tell him it was one long bore, now I know what happiness . . .'

LULU: I'm not selling the only thing I've ever owned!

CASTI-PIANI: You haven't heard the rest, let me go on.

LULU: I'll give you everything.

CASTI-PIANI: I've had everything. If you haven't left with me by eleven, I'll have the whole pack of you deported to Germany.

LULU: You wouldn't betray me!

CASTI-PIANI: Why not? Do you think that's the worst thing I've ever done in my life? I must have a word with Bianetta in case we do leave.

    CASTI-PIANI *goes into the gaming room leaving the door half open.* LULU *convulsively crumples* RODRIGO'S *note which she has been holding in her hand throughout the previous scene.*

LULU (*savagely*): A brothel.

    Becoming conscious of the note for the first time she reads it. She starts laughing wildly.

ALWA *runs in excitedly from the gaming room clutching some bankers' shares and money.*

ALWA: I'm doing brilliantly. Puntschu has promised me ten more Virgin shares. Steinherz's winning too but Geschwitz has been wiped out. Why aren't you playing?

LULU: I will.

ALWA: By the way, it's in today's *Berliner Tagenblatt* – Alfred Hugenburg threw himself over the prison stairs.

LULU: Was he in prison too?

But ALWA *is too eager to go back into the gaming room to answer.* LULU *moves to follow him.* GESCHWITZ *meets her in the doorway.*

GESCHWITZ: Are you going because I'm coming?

LULU (*exasperated*): No!

GESCHWITZ (*quickly closing the door*): You've cheated me out of everything I own. You might at least keep up a show of civility when you're with me.

LULU: I'm as civil to you as I am with any woman.

GESCHWITZ: I was imprisoned for your sake. What about all those promises we made when we were in hospital?

LULU: I promised a lot of things. Why did you give me cholera?

GESCHWITZ (*sobbing*): You tricked me.

LULU: And you've tricked me. You've seduced one of my admirers with your airs and graces.

GESCHWITZ: Admirer? Me?

LULU (*mocking*): Your acrobat, Rodrigo Quast. You don't know how lucky you are. He can balance two cavalry horses on his chest – *saddled*!

GESCHWITZ: You know just how to torture your slaves. But I don't envy you. My pain's nothing to what you must suffer with Casti-Piani.

LULU (*suddenly furious*): Don't you dare say a word about him! He loves me. He makes your sacrifices look pathetic. He's made me see what a pervert you are. Go to Miss Bianetta. She'll do anything if she's paid!

Suddenly BIANETTA, MAGELONE, LUDMILLA, CASTI-PIANI, PUNSCHU, HEILMAN, *and* ALWA *all come in from the gaming room laughing and talking.* LULU *breaks away from* GESCHWITZ.

LULU: What's happened?

BIANETTA: I must've won a fortune.

ALWA: I've got 40,000 shares.

MAGELONE: Everybody's winning!

ALWA: Where does all the money come from?

CASTI-PIANI: It doesn't do to ask. It's enough to know we shan't be short of champagne.

ALWA: Let's go to supper, ladies – to supper!

Laughing and talking the whole company go into the dining room Stage Left. RODRIGO *detains* LULU.

RODRIGO: One moment, beloved. Did you read my little billet-doux?

LULU (*throwing the note at him*): It's no good you threatening me with the police. There's no money left.

RODRIGO: Don't lie to me, you bitch! Your husband has 40,000 shares.

LULU: Blackmail *him* then!

RODRIGO: Thanks for the permission. It takes forty-eight hours for that blockhead to understand anything. By the time he gets the point my fiancée'll have broken off our engagement.

LULU (*about to leave, stops*): You're engaged?

RODRIGO: I suppose I should've asked your permission first? That's my thanks for getting you out of prison and ruining my health. Do you realize the first evening I appeared on stage in my new strong-man act some lout in the audience threw an armchair at me? The French are too decadent to understand genuine feats of strength. If I were a boxing kangaroo I'd be interviewed – have my picture in the papers. Thanks to my fiancée I don't have to worry about that any more. Her name is Celestine and she has thirty years' savings deposited at the National Bank. And she loves me for my own sake. She isn't just interested in obscenities like you. She has three children by an American bishop and great things are expected of them. We're being married the day after tomorrow.

LULU: Then what do you want my money for?

RODRIGO: I told my fiancée I had 20,000.

LULU (*laughing*): And she loves you for your own sake.

RODRIGO (*drawing himself up with dignity*): My fiancée admires me as a man of feeling, not as a man of strength like you and your crowd. That's all over and done with.

LULU: Then why the devil are you pestering poor Geschwitz?

RODRIGO (*indignant*): I'm not! I've only been talking to her. She's an aristocrat and I'm a man of the world and I know more about elegant conversation than the whole bloody lot of you. Are you going to give me the money by tomorrow evening or not?

LULU: I'm broke.

RODRIGO: You think I've got chicken-shit for brains! That husband of yours would give you his last penny even though you shot his father. But you've got to be faithful to him. If you're going to sacrifice yourself, sacrifice yourself to some purpose. Make four people happy. But no. It's always Casti-Piani, Casti-Piani!

LULU: Shall I ask him to throw you out?

RODRIGO: As you please. But if I don't have 20,000 by tomorrow night, I'll report you to the police, m'lady.

As LULU *storms out to the dining room with* RODRIGO *following her,* PUNTSCHU *passes them.*

PUNTSCHU: It's hot in there.

They don't answer him as they exit. He looks after them, shrugs and sits.

(*musing*) I must unload those J. T. Thomas shares. . . . One always has to keep thinking . . . no time to rest . . .

BOB *a thirteen-year-old groom in red jacket, light leather breeches and glistening boots enters Stage Right. He hands* PUNTSCHU *a telegram.*

BOB: For you, sir.

PUNTSCHU (*opens telegram, reads*: Hhhmmm . . . Virgin shares *fallen* . . . ah well . . . way of the world . . .

(BOB *is moving away;* PUNTSCHU *gives him a tip.*)
What's your name, lad?

BOB: Freddy. But they call me Bob because it's the fashion.

PUNTSCHU *suddenly pulls him close; he struggles as* KADIDJA *enters uncertainly from the dining room.*

KADIDJA: Have you seen Mama?

PUNTSCHU: No, my child . . . (*Pulls her to him with free hand; she struggles.*) Ah what breeding . . . Your mama'll be back shortly . . . (*Turns back to* BOB) What beautiful knee breeches . . . hhmm . . . hhmm . . .

The two children manage to break away.

KADIDJA: Have *you* seen my Mama?

BOB: She went up in the lift. Come on. We can hide in the corridor and . . .

MAGELONE comes through the Stage door Right, seizes KADIDJA.

KADIDJA: I've been looking for you, Mama.

MAGELONE: Who told you to! What you been doing with this boy? You wretched little . . .

KADIDJA is thrown on the floor and starts crying as HEILMAN, ALWA, LUDMILLA, GESCHWITZ, *and* LULU *come in from the dining room.* BOB *discreetly exits as they crowd round* KADIDJA.

MAGELONE: Stop it!

LULU: Why are you crying, sweetheart?

LUDMILLA: Tell me, angel, what nasty thing happened? Would you like some cake?

MAGELONE: It's her nerves. The child's developing them far too early.

PUNTSCHU: You're an unnatural mother. The courts will take the child away from you and appoint me her guardian. Won't they my little goddess? (*He picks up the screaming* KADIDJA *and carries her laughing into the gaming room.*)

GESCHWITZ: What a relief. We can start playing baccarat again.

As the company move back into the gaming room BOB *re-enters and whispers something to* LULU. *She nods and then kisses him passionately on the mouth.*

LULU closes the door to the gaming room as BOB *ushers in* SCHIGOLCH *Stage Right. He is wearing a dress coat, worn patent-leather shoes and a battered opera hat which he keeps on.*

SCHIGOLCH (*glances after* BOB): Where did you get him?

LULU: From the circus.

SCHIGOLCH (*smiling*): What are his wages?

LULU: Why don't you ask him!

SCHIGOLCH *sits with a sigh.*

SCHIGOLCH: The fact is, I need money. I've just taken an apartment here for my mistress. She's from Frankfurt. She used to be the wife of the King of Naples. She was very captivating when she was young – so she keeps telling me.

LULU (*crossing to him calmly*): Do you need much?

SCHIGOLCH: Nothing. A mere trifle. She wants . . .

LULU *suddenly lets out a howl and falls at* SCHIGOLCH's *feet weeping.*

SCHIGOLCH (*patting her*): There, there, what's the matter?

LULU (*crying*): God . . . God . . . God . . .

SCHIGOLCH (*pulling her on to his lap, holding her like a child*): You really ought to go to bed early with a good book – for once in your life . . . that's right, have a good cry . . . I remember you like this fifteen years ago . . . how you screamed . . . but you didn't have no white feathers in your head then, or stockings.

LULU (*howling*): Take me home with you tonight . . . please . . . please . . .

SCHIGOLCH: I'll take you home with me. I'll take you home . . .

LULU: They're going to hand me over to the police.

SCHIGOLCH: Who's going to?

LULU: The acrobat, Rodrigo Quast.

SCHIGOLCH (*quietly*): I'll deal with him.

LULU (*imploring like a child*): Yes, you deal with him.

SCHIGOLCH: If he comes to my hotel – *phut*! My window opens on to the river. But he won't come.

LULU: What's your number?

SCHIGOLCH: 376, Hotel France. The last building before the Hippodrome.

LULU: He'll be there. With that idiot woman who keeps crawling round my feet. You'd better go and get things ready. When it's done, bring me the gold ring he wears in his ear. It'll be easy, he doesn't notice things when he's drunk.

SCHIGOLCH: And after . . .?

LULU: I'll give you money for your lady friend . . . (SCHIGOLCH *shakes his head.*) Anything then . . .

SCHIGOLCH: We haven't been together for ten years.

LULU (*laughing*): Is that all. (*Kisses him.*) But you have a mistress.

SCHIGOLCH: My lady friend from Frankfurt is not in the first flush of youth.

LULU: You must swear you'll do it.

SCHIGOLCH: Have I ever broken my word to you?

LULU: Swear you'll deal with him!

SCHIGOLCH (*quietly*): I'll deal with him.

LULU: Swear! SWEAR!

   SCHIGOLCH *pulls up her dress and lays his hand on her crutch.*

SCHIGOLCH: By all that's holy, I swear.

LULU: By all that's holy . . . how cool that feels.

SCHIGOLCH: It has the opposite effect on me.

   LULU *gets off his lap.*

LULU: You must be ready for them.

SCHIGOLCH (*heaving himself to his feet*): I'm going. (LULU *suddenly stares at him and shudders violently.*) Why are you looking at me like that? (LULU *doesn't answer.*) Are you dumb? What's the matter?

LULU: My garter just broke.

SCHIGOLCH: Oh, is that all.

LULU: What does it mean?

SCHIGOLCH: *Mean?* It means I'll fasten it for you, if you stand still.

LULU: It means bad luck.

SCHIGOLCH: Not for you, child . . . Don't worry I'll deal with him.

   As LULU *goes out with* SCHIGOLCH *Stage Right* CASTI-PIANI *propels* RODRIGO *in from the dining room.*

RODRIGO: Lout!

CASTI-PIANI: You threatened to denounce her.

RODRIGO: Liar!

CASTI-PIANI: She told me! You threatened to denounce her to the police if she didn't go upstairs with you.

RODRIGO: If I wanted her to go with me, she'd go like that. I wouldn't have to threaten her with prison.

CASTI-PIANI (*taking out watch*): Eleven o'clock. You're too late. I have some business to attend to.

He exits into the gaming room.

RODRIGO (*recovering*): Come back and I'll twist your guts round your neck . . . (LULU *returns*.) What's the idea of telling him I wanted to seduce you, you bitch!

LULU: Geschwitz is in a terrible state. She'll jump in the river if she's kept waiting any longer.

RODRIGO: What's the old cow waiting for?

LULU: You.

RODRIGO: Tell her she'd better jump.

LULU: She has 20,000 marks. If you go away with her they'll be deposited in your name at any bank you choose.

RODRIGO: And if I don't go?

LULU: You'll have to denounce me. Alwa and I are cleaned out.

RODRIGO: Judas!

LULU: Stop being so particular. If you're going to sacrifice yourself, sacrifice yourself to some purpose, make four people happy.

RODRIGO: No it won't work. I was only interested in talking to her because I realized she's an aristocrat and I'm a gentleman. (*He pulls the cork out of a bottle with his teeth, spits it out and pours a drink.*)

LULU: The Countess is waiting. What shall I tell her?

RODRIGO: I'm homosexual.

LULU (*moving away*): Very well.

RODRIGO: Hold on. Are you certain I'll get the 20,000?

LULU: Ask her yourself.

RODRIGO (*grimly*): All right I'm ready.

LULU: Where will you be?

RODRIGO: I'll wait for her in the dining room. I'd better fortify myself with a bucketful of oysters first.

He goes into the dining room. LULU *opens the gaming room door, beckons and calls 'Martha'.* GESCHWITZ *comes in closing the doors behind her.*

LULU: Darling, I'm so sorry for what I said before. Forgive me, darling.

GESCHWITZ: I always forgive you.

LULU: My darling you can save my life.

GESCHWITZ: How my love?

LULU: By going to a brothel with our acrobat.

GESCHWITZ: *What?* Why?

LULU: He says he must have you tonight or he'll denounce me to the police.

GESCHWITZ: You know I can't go with a man.

LULU: He's fallen in love with you.

GESCHWITZ: He's an animal. He'll be disappointed and then he'll try to break my neck. It's happened to me before.

LULU: What will you get out of it if I'm denounced.

GESCHWITZ: I've still got enough money for us to travel to America, steerage. You'd be safe there.

LULU: I like it here. All you have to do is flatter him. Tell the cab driver to take you to the Hotel France, Room 376. They'll be expecting you for the evening.

GESCHWITZ: How can it save you?

LULU (*craftily*): It will and it might even cure you.

GESCHWITZ (*sighing*): Oh Lulu I hope you'll never be judged. I can't believe there's no God – but why should he make an insignificant worm like me suffer so much?

LULU: You've nothing to complain about. When you are happy you're a thousand times happier than us normal people.

GESCHWITZ: Perhaps I am. I'm not complaining but you've deceived me so many times.

LULU (*holding her hands*): Keep the acrobat quiet tonight and I'm yours.

GESCHWITZ: And tomorrow?

LULU (*drawing her close*): I'll wait for you, my darling. I shan't open my eyes till you come to me. (*They kiss.*)

GESCHWITZ (*ecstatically*): Yes . . . oh, yes . . .

LULU: Don't forget. Throw yourself at him. You've got the number – 376.

GESCHWITZ: Be quick, my love.

LULU *calls into the dining room.*

LULU: Rodrigo . . .!

RODRIGO *enters eating. He sees* GESCHWITZ, *shudders and braces himself.*

RODRIGO: Sorry . . . ladies . . . mouth full . . .

GESCHWITZ (*holding out her hand*): I adore you! Take pity on me.

RODRIGO (*wiping his mouth with his sleeve*): Ah la bonne heure! (*kisses her hand*) This way to the execution!

He burps and offers GESCHWITZ *his arm, and they exit Stage Right.* LULU *accompanies them to the door and calls after them.*

LULU: Good night, children . . . (*calling, low, urgent*) Bob! Quick! (BOB *appears in the doorway.*) What time is it?

BOB: Just gone eleven.

LULU: I'm leaving. You come with me.

BOB: As Madame wishes.

LULU: You can stop calling me Madame. We'll exchange clothes. Hurry.

As they rush away there is a loud commotion in the gaming room. The doors are flung open and PUNTSCHU, HEILMAN, ALWA, BIANETTA, MAGELONE, KADIDJA, *and* LUDMILLA *pour in.*

HEILMAN (*clutching shares*): Why won't you accept these Virgin shares, Sir!

PUNTSCHU: Because the stock has no official quotation.

HEILMAN: Give me a chance to get my own back!

MAGELONE: What is it?

BIANETTA: Puntschu has won all the cash and has given up the game.

LUDMILLA: The stinking Jew's got cold feet.

PUNTSCHU: Who says I've got cold feet? But the gentleman must bet cash. Not worthless bits of paper.

HEILMAN: Worthless bits . . . but these shares stand at 210 . . .

PUNTSCHU: Yesterday they stood at 210. Today they're not standing at all. Tomorrow you can paper the walls with 'em.

ALWA: I'm finished!

PUNTSCHU: So am I. I've lost my entire fortune. And tomorrow morning I'll have the pleasure of starting to make it again from scratch.

MAGELONE (*dazed*): Have the Virgin shares fallen?

PUNTSCHU: Even further than you have, Madame.

MAGELONE: Ahhhh! (*She faints.*)

KADIDJA: Mama! Mama; wake up!

BIANETTA: Tell me, Herr Puntschu, where are you going to dine this evening, now that you're wiped out?

PUNTSCHU (*gallantly*): Wherever you like, Madamoiselle. Wherever you like. But let's decide outside. The atmosphere's becoming a trifle strained in here.

> PUNTSCHU *offers* BIANETTA *his arm, she steps over the prostrate form of* MAGELONE *and they exit through the gaming room.*

> HEILMAN *tears up his shares and stamps on them in fury.*

HEILMAN: That's what one gets for associating with such scum.

LUDMILLA: You're a journalist. Why don't you send an article to the French police about this little group?

HEILMAN (*stops stamping*): Hmmm. Yes . . .

LUDMILLA: I know a café open all night. Between the two of us we should be able to produce something by morning.

HEILMAN: Don't you ever sleep?

LUDMILLA: Of course. But not at night.

> *They exit Stage Right, whilst* KADIDJA *and* ALWA *are left crouched over* MAGELONE. ALWA *slaps her hands, trying to bring her round.*

ALWA: Her hands are as cold as ice. (*Peers closer.*) Magnificent looking woman. Kadidja, help me undo your mother's bodice.

> LULU *rushes in Stage Right in* BOB'S *red jacket, knee breeches, top boots.* BOB *reluctantly shuffles in beside her dressed in her white Directoire gown and a white shawl over his head.*

LULU: Have you any cash, Alwa?

ALWA (*up*): Have you gone mad?

LULU: We've been denounced. The police'll be here any second. You can stay if you want!

ALWA: Not me!

> *They rush out together Stage Right after pushing* BOB *on to the love-seat.*

70

KADIDJA (*shaking* MAGELONE): Mama, Mama, they're all gone
 . . . Mama!

*MAGELONE regains consciousness groaning. She sees BOB
hunched on the love-seat and screams. At that moment a French
POLICEMAN bursts in Stage Centre with CASTI-PIANI.
MAGELONE screams again and faints.*

POLICEMAN: Countess Adelaide d'Oubre alias Mignon Schön.
 I arrest you in the name of the law . . .

*A pause. Then CASTI-PIANI snatches away the shawl to reveal
BOB's frightened features looking up at the POLICEMAN.*

CASTI-PIANI: Yes there is something wrong with the whole
 system.

*Distorted circus music plays over. Lights out. Music continues,
then a tremendous crash as someone is hurled through plate glass, a
falling cry 'Ahhhhhhh!' followed by a loud splash. Silence.*

SCENE THREE

*A barrel organ plays 'There'll Always be an England', and Spot up
on a large shattered distorting mirror. LULU in a torn black dress,
hair loose, stands soliciting in front of it, hand on hip. Spot out.*

 *Lights up on a basement room formerly groom's quarters with
halters and straps on the walls and straw on the floor. It is completely
broken down.*

 *Up Stage Centre entrance door. Stage Right a cubby-hole, Stage
Left a room off. Up Stage Right a battered chaise-longue. Down
Stage Right a rickety flower-stand with a bottle and a paraffin
lamp. Stage Left a broken chair.*

 *ALWA is huddled on the chaise-longue wrapped in a rug.
SCHIGOLCH in a long, grey overcoat lies on a torn mattress
Down Stage Left.*

SCHIGOLCH: Hark at that rain.

ALWA: Very appropriate weather for her début. I was dreaming
 we were dining together in the Olympic Rooms – the table
 dripping with champagne . . .

SCHIGOLCH: I was dreaming of Christmas pudding.

    LULU *enters Stage Left.*

LULU: If only I could warm myself up on one of you two.

ALWA (*bitterly*): Are you going to start your pilgrimage tonight?

SCHIGOLCH: The first step always means a lot of moaning and groaning. It was the same twenty years ago with her, and she's come a long way since then. The fire needs fanning, that's all. Wait till she's been at it a week, you won't be able to keep her indoors.

LULU: It's stopped raining.

SCHIGOLCH: You should be out on the streets then.

LULU: I wish I could sleep for ever.

ALWA: So do I. Let's kill ourselves tonight. Starve ourselves to death. It's how we'll end up anyway.

LULU: Why don't you go out and work so we can eat?

ALWA: In weather like this?

LULU: But you expect me to.

ALWA: I won't touch a penny of your money.

SCHIGOLCH: Let her go. I want a taste of Christmas pudding, then I'll die happy.

ALWA: I'd like a beefsteak and a cigarette . . .

SCHIGOLCH: She'd rather see us die than let herself have a bit of fun. *Selfish!*

LULU: I'd like to meet the woman who could earn a living with the rags I've got on.

ALWA (*scrambling up*): I've tried everything! I spent night after night working out a foolproof gambling system didn't I? And I offered myself to women, didn't I?

SCHIGOLCH: Yes, yes.

ALWA: They didn't even laugh at my jokes. They didn't want to get involved with someone with a police record.

SCHIGOLCH: It's time you were going, child, I've an idea I shan't grow old in these lodgings. My toes've been numb for weeks (*rubs his hands*). I'm going upstairs for a couple of drinks, later. The landlady told me yesterday I've a good chance of becoming her lover.

72

LULU (*picking up the bottle*): What the devil! I'm going out! (*she drinks*).

SCHIGOLCH: Stop it. Your customers'll smell your breath half a mile away.

ALWA: You're not going, I forbid it!

LULU: You can't forbid anything, you can't even feed me.

ALWA (*slumping in chair*): And who's fault is it? Who dragged me through the mud. You and that damned Casti-Piani of yours.

LULU (*shivering*): It's cold . . . There's nothing sadder in the world than a woman of joy.

SCHIGOLCH: Patience, patience. Business'll soon pick up.

LULU: It's all the same to me. What does it matter . . .
She exits Up Stage Centre.

ALWA: She could've been the Empress of Russia, another Catherine the Great . . . We grew up together you know.

SCHIGOLCH: She'll outlive us all.

ALWA: She went to the Spanish Ambassador's Ball in pink tulle – nothing underneath but a bodice of white lace. Dr Goll begged me to dance with her to prevent possible indiscretions. Father didn't take his eyes off us and all through the waltz. She kept looking at him over my shoulder. Later she shot him of course.

SCHIGOLCH (*getting up*): I don't think anyone will bite tonight.

ALWA: She really understood the art of listening. From being my little sister she became my stepmother, then my mistress. That the way it is . . .

SCHIGOLCH: She's quite liable to turn down a good solid gentleman with money for some penniless tramp she's taken a fancy to.

ALWA: Even when she was in my father's arms her thoughts turned to me. And it couldn't have happened that often; he was past his prime and she was betraying him with the game-keeper. (*Footsteps off.*)

SCHIGOLCH: Here they are.

ALWA (*jumping up*): I won't stand for it. I'll throw him out.
With an effort SCHIGOLCH *propels* ALWA *across Stage Right.*

SCHIGOLCH: No man'd feel at ease with us two lying about.

SCHIGOLCH shoves ALWA through the door Stage Right and follows him into the cubby hole.

ALWA (*off*): I'll hear everything.

SCHIGOLCH (*off*): Be quiet!

ALWA (*off*): I'll kill him.

LULU enters Up Stage Centre with a deaf mute, MR HUNIDEI, a large man with a rosy face and friendly smile. He wears coat, top hat and carries a dripping umbrella.

LULU: This is where I live.

HUNIDEI puts his forefinger to his mouth looks meaningly at LULU.

It isn't very cosy. (*HUNIDEI puts his hand over her mouth.*) . . . What is it? (*Puts his left hand over her mouth again.*) No one can hear us, we're alone.

HUNIDEI puts his forefinger to his lips and ears and shakes his head making strange rasping noises. Touching LULU's lips he shakes his head again, indicating he doesn't want her to speak. Taking off his coat he lays it carefully on the chair.

(*to herself*): Good God he's a freak.

SCHIGOLCH slightly opens the door Stage Right and peers out.

SCHIGOLCH: He's got a screw loose.

ALWA (*head appearing*): I'll kill him.

They both disappear as HUNIDEI comes back to LULU to kiss her.

LULU: I hope you're going to give me something.

HUNIDEI gives her a gold coin. She looks at it, then at him. He looks uncertain.

LULU: I suppose it's enough.

HUNIDEI gives her a few silver coins.

(*nodding*) That's good of you.

HUNIDEI gives an inarticulate cry of delight and grabs LULU. She leads him to the room Stage Left grunting and crying. ALWA and SCHIGOLCH creep out of their cubby-hole on all fours.

ALWA: I can't hear anything.

SCHIGOLCH: Careful.

ALWA: I'll listen by the door.

SCHIGOLCH: Milk-sop.

He pushes past ALWA, *gropes for* HUNIDEI'S *coat and goes through the pockets.*

SCHIGOLCH (*disgusted*): Nothing . . . (*He finds a book in the inside pocket.*) What is it?

ALWA (*coming back and holds the book to the light: reading title*): 'Exhortations to Pious Pilgrims, by Rev. J. Arnold. Price 2/6.'

SCHIGOLCH: There's nothing you can do with the English. As a nation their best days are over.

ALWA: It's never as bad as one thinks it's going to be.

SCHIGOLCH: He hadn't even got a silk scarf. And these are the people we crawl on our bellies to in Germany . . . She couldn't have brought back anyone more pathetic.

They creep back into their cubby-hole as LULU *comes out of her room followed by* HUNIDEI.

LULU: Will you come again?

HUNIDEI *picks up his coat and umbrella and leaves briskly Up Stage Centre without looking at her.*

SCHIGOLCH *and* ALWA *emerge.*

LULU: He was quite exciting . . .

ALWA: How much did he give you?

LULU: Here take it. I'm going out again.

SCHIGOLCH (*taking coins*): We can live like princes.

Footsteps off.

ALWA: He's coming back.

LULU (*listening*): It's not him.

Knocking on the door.

SCHIGOLCH: He must've recommended a friend. You see that's how business grows!

LULU: Come in.

COUNTESS GESCHWITZ *enters poorly dressed and carrying a rolled canvas.*

GESCHWITZ: If this is inconvenient I'll go. I didn't get the money. My brother didn't even reply.

SCHIGOLCH: So now you want to sponge off us?

LULU: I'm going down again.

GESCHWITZ: I've brought you something. On my way here a dealer offered me twelve shillings. But I couldn't part with it.

ALWA *takes the canvas from her and unrolls it on the floor.*
ALWA: It's Lulu's portrait.
LULU (*screaming with rage*): Yaaarrrrhhhh! You brought it here! Throw it away!
ALWA (*rejuvenated as he studies the painting*): Yes, yes, now I see why! Now I understand how I allowed her to do this to me! I can understand what happened to me! No one nowhere could feel safe in front of those lips, those eyes, that pink ripe body, NO ONE . . .
SCHIGOLCH: Let's hang it up. It'll make an excellent impression on our clientele.

   ALWA *excitedly fastens the picture on the wall.*
GESCHWITZ: I cut it out of the frame after you all left the house.
ALWA: A pity the paint's flaking at the edges. You didn't roll it carefully enough!
SCHIGOLCH: It gives the whole place an air of elegance.
ALWA: Her beauty was at its height when that was painted. In spite of everything she's been through the eyes are still the same . . . But the freshness of her skin then, the fragrance round her lips, the whiteness of her neck and arms, the golden splendour of her flesh . . .
SCHIGOLCH: All in the ash can. (*gesturing to painting*) But at least she can say, 'that's what I was once'. It's lucky though at this time of night customers aren't concerned so much with physical charms; they pick the least mercenary-looking pair of eyes.
LULU: Well I'll go out again and see if you're right.
ALWA (*suddenly raging*): You're not going out again!
GESCHWITZ (*to* LULU): Where are you going?
ALWA: To pick up a man.
GESCHWITZ: Lulu!
ALWA: She's done it once tonight already.
GESCHWITZ (*holding* LULU): Lulu . . . I'll go with you.
SCHIGOLCH: Find your own beat!
GESCHWITZ: I shan't leave your side, Lulu. I'm armed.
SCHIGOLCH: She's trying to fish with our bait.

76

LULU: I can't bear it!

GESCHWITZ: Don't be afraid. I'm with you, darling.

   LULU *rushes off Up Stage Centre followed by* GESCHWITZ.

SCHIGOLCH: We ought to have held that damned woman back
   by the throat. She'll scare off every customer in miles . . .
   (*Goes back to his mattress and lies down.*) But I must say she's
   got guts enough for ten men. If she hadn't enticed that bone-
   headed, jumping-jack Rodrigo to my room that night we'd
   still have him round our necks. Turn down the lamp a bit.

   ALWA *gets up, crosses and turns down the lamp.*

ALWA: What a mess I've made of my life.

SCHIGOLCH: What a mess this filthy weather's made of my
   coat. When I was young I knew how to look after myself.

ALWA: I deliberately sought out the company of people who'd
   never read a book in their lives. I thought they'd enrich my
   poetry. I was wrong. Since my father's death I haven't written
   a line. I'm a martyr to my profession.

SCHIGOLCH: I hope they haven't stayed together. Nobody but
   an idiot goes with a pair at night. (*Footsteps off.*) She's coming
   back. (*Scrambles up.*)

ALWA: I'm staying here. I haven't the energy . . . I'm not going
   to let my comfort be disturbed.

   *He creeps back to the chaise-longue and pulls the rug completely
   over him.*

SCHIGOLCH: A man of sense accepts his situation.

   He crawls back into the cubby-hole Stage Right. LULU *enters
   Up Stage Centre.*

LULU: Come in, darling.

   KUNGU POTI, *Crown Prince of Uahubee, enters in a light-
   coloured coat, light trousers, white spats and yellow buttoned boots.
   He carries a heavy knobbly stick.*

KUNGU: God damn . . . is very dark on stairs.

LULU: It's lighter in here, sweetheart.

KUNGU: 'Tis cold here . . .

LULU: Have some brandy. (*Gives him bottle.*)

KUNGU: Always I drink brandy. Brandy is good. (*Drinks.*)
   Plenty brandy.

LULU: You're a pretty young fellow.

KUNGU: My father is King of Uahubee. I have six wives. 'Cause I's going to be d'coming King . . .

LULU: How much are you going to give me?

KUNGU: Always give gold pieces. Me never pay first.

LULU: At least let me see it.

KUNGU: No understand!

LULU: Let me see the money!

KUNGU: No understand! Come!

He suddenly seizes LULU *round the waist. Surprised she struggles and shouts to tear herself free.* ALWA *creeps up behind* KUNGU *and hauls him back by the coat collar.*

KUNGU: 'Tis a den of murderers . . . give you sleep-medicine. (*He smashes* ALWA *across the head with his stick.* ALWA *collapses with a groan.*) Nice dreams waiting . . . d'coming King goes!

He exits with LULU *running after him.*

LULU: Come back.

SCHIGOLCH *emerges from his cubby-hole.*

SCHIGOLCH: Alwa . . . (*Bends over him.*) Look alive there . . . (*Touches his head.*) Blood . . . Alwa! You can't just lie here, you'll disturb the customers . . . Alwa! . . . Probably want to sleep it off . . .

Taking ALWA *by the scruff of the neck, he hauls him into* LULU'S *room Stage Left.*

SCHIGOLCH (*returning*): Time for my drink. (*His eyes fall on* LULU'S *portrait.*) She's hopeless. Doesn't understand a thing. She'll never make a living out of love because making love is her life. *Amateur.* (*Footsteps off.*) That's her. I'll try one last appeal to her conscience.

But COUNTESS GESCHWITZ *enters.*

SCHIGOLCH: Oh it's you.

GESCHWITZ: She doesn't want me.

SCHIGOLCH (*irritably*): If you're going to stay here the night make yourself useful and see nothing gets pinched. Alwa's gone to bed. If anyone should ask for me I'm upstairs having a drink and, I hope, a slice of Christmas pudding.

He exits. GESCHWITZ *takes the cane chair and sits in shadows by the wall.*

GESCHWITZ (*dully*): I'll watch without flinching . . . They eat, drink and make love . . . I wonder if anyone's ever been made happy by love. Doesn't their happiness consist of being able to sleep better and forget everything? (*quietly*) Lord God, I thank thee for not being like other women . . . but I suffer, my soul is shrivelled up with pain . . . and I know the sacrifice is worthless . . .

Footsteps. LULU *enters with* DR HILTI. GESCHWITZ *remains seated in the shadows; they don't notice her.*

LULU (*gaily*): You'll stay the night with me.

DR HILTI: I only have five shillings.

LULU: That's enough. Because it's you. You have such beautiful eyes. Kiss me!

HILTI: Jesus, Mary, Joseph . . . This is the first time I've ever been with a woman.

LULU: Aren't you married?

DR HILTI: Of course not. I'm a University lecturer.

LULU: So that's why you've never had a woman before.

DR HILTI: But I've got to have one now. I was officially engaged to a girl from Basle this evening.

LULU: Is she pretty?

DR HILTI: Yes, she has two million. (*putting arm round her waist*) I can hardly wait to see what it's like.

LULU (*delighted throwing back her hair*): A virgin! I'm so lucky. If you're ready, Professor?

She conducts DR HILTI *into her room. As the door closes* GESCHWITZ *stands up, takes a small black revolver from her pocket and points it dramatically at her head. There is a cry of fright from* LULU'S *room. The door is dragged open and* DR HILTI *staggers out followed by* LULU *with the lamp.*

DR HILTI: There's a dead body!

LULU (*clutching his arm*): Stay with me.

DR HILTI: It's filthy . . . (*He sees* GESCHWITZ *with the gun.* Arrrrkk!

LULU: Stay with me.

DR HILTI (*rushes away*): My God – it's a filthy business!
He rushes out.

LULU: Stop . . . (*to* GESCHWITZ) Now look what you've done!
She runs out after DR HILTI.

GESCHWITZ: If she saw me lying dead she wouldn't weep. It's
better if I jumped into the river. Which is colder? . . . the
water or her heart? Better hang myself . . . before she comes
back . . . (*She takes a strap from the wall and climbs on to the chair.*)
I often dreamed we were kissing, then I woke up . . . better to
hang . . . not the river, water is too pure for me . . . (*She puts
the strap round her neck.*) Quickly before she comes back . . .
quickly . . . quickly . . . (*She fastens the end of the strap to a hook
in the wall, closes her eyes and kicks the chair away. But the hook
breaks and she falls on to the floor. She opens her eyes.*)
Damn . . . I'm alive . . . Perhaps I'm not meant to die . . .
perhaps I can still be happy. Lulu . . . Lulu . . . (*She crosses to
LULU's portrait and sinks to her knees in front of it.*) My angel . . .
my star . . . have pity on me . . .

LULU *enters with* JACK. *He has thick eyebrows, a drooping
moustache and hands spotted with red hair. His movements are
elastic but his eyes are fixed on the ground. He wears a dark
overcoat.*

JACK (*seeing* GESCHWITZ): Who's this?

LULU: My sister. She's mad. I don't know what to do with her.

JACK (*to* LULU): You have a pretty mouth – how much? I've
no money left.

LULU: I'm not asking for much. Just a little something.

JACK (*turning to go*): Good evening!

LULU (*holding him back*): No, no, stay till morning for God's
sake.

JACK (*pacing, sniffing*): Why should I? – it sounds suspicious –
when I'm asleep you'll rob me.

LULU: I wouldn't do that. Please stay.

JACK: How much do you want?

LULU: Half of what I asked before.

JACK: Still too much . . . (*Pauses.*) You don't seem t've been at
this game very long.

LULU: Tonight's the first time.

GESCHWITZ *still on her knees, has half risen to* JACK. LULU *pulls her back by the strap, still round her neck.*

LULU: Will you lie down!

JACK: Let her alone. She's not your sister, she's in love with you . . . (*He pulls on* GESCHWITZ'S *strap as if she were a dog.*) There girl . . . there . . . there. (*He suddenly looks up.*)

LULU: Why are you staring at me like that?

JACK: You have a pretty mouth. I've only got a silver piece on me.

LULU: Oh what does it matter? Give it to me.

JACK: I want some change for the bus fare home in the morning

LULU: I haven't any change.

JACK: Go through your pockets – there – let me see.

LULU (*showing him a coin*): It's too much. I'll give you half tomorrow.

JACK: No – I want it all.

LULU (*thrusting it at him*): Oh all right. Now come on for God's sake.

She is about to go into her room when she remembers ALWA *is in there. Instead she picks up the lamp and heads for the cubby-hole Stage Right.*

JACK: We don't need any light, the moon's shining.

LULU *puts down the lamp, throws her arms round* JACK.

LULU: I won't hurt you. I like you so much.

JACK: I'm ready.

LULU *leads him by the hand into the cubby-hole.*

GESCHWITZ (*undoing the strap*): I'll go back home . . . Mother will send me the fare . . . I'll study law and fight for women's rights . . .

A terrible scream off. LULU *in her petticoat runs out screaming.*

LULU (*hysterical*): Help me! Help me!

GESCHWITZ *rushes over with her revolver and she pushes* LULU *behind her as* JACK *bent double, his face painted white, comes out roaring and plunges a knife into* GESCHWITZ'S *stomach; she fires but hits the ceiling as she collapses.* JACK *snatches the gun from her and hurls himself bodily at the nearest wall firing the gun wildly.*

JACK: Pretty mouth! Pretty mouth!

He slashes the air in front of LULU'S *picture.* LULU *picks up a bottle smashes it against the table and rushes at* JACK *with the broken-off neck in her hand. Grabbing her wrist* JACK *sends the broken bottle flying across the room and picks her up bodily.*

LULU: Help me! (*He carries her into the cubby-hole screaming.*) Help me! Help me!

A crescendo of screams. An unnaturally loud tearing sound. Silence . . . Then JACK'S *orgastic cries are heard. He staggers out.*

JACK: I'm so lucky . . . I'm so lucky . . . (*As in a dream he slowly raises the bloodstained knife high like a chalice and licks it. A pause then his manner changes abruptly. He crosses briskly to the wash basin whistling* 'Land of Hope and Glory'. *He washes his face, hands and knife and looks around.*) Miserable hole. They haven't even got a towel. (*He crosses menacingly to* GESCHWITZ, *bends down and wipes the knife on her dress; to her*) Monster . . . You haven't got long either. (*He puts the knife away, goes to the door and pauses.*) A good night's work.

He exits. Lights dim down to a Spot on GESCHWITZ, *lying clutching her stomach.*

GESCHWITZ: Lulu . . . Lulu . . . My dream . . . Lulu . . . Lulu . . .
She dies. Spot fades out. Circus music. Darkness.

CURTAIN